Spinning Plates

Tips, Thoughts and Ideas for Balancing Work, Parenting and Home

by

Penny Clayton

and

Wendy Reus

Setting, design & illustrations: Simon Clayton

To our inspirational mothers who helped us believe in ourselves.

Spinning Plates

Contents

Acknowledgements

Introduction, p.11

Why we wrote this book and what it covers. How it is set out and a bit about us.

Chapter 1 Being Pregnant and Working, p.17

Tips for working when pregnant. Employer's perspective. How to look after yourself. Looking after your emotional needs. Keeping your relationships healthy. Practical tips to make life easier. Helping children adapt to the changes.

Chapter 2 Arranging Child Care, p.43

Childcare: advantages and disadvantages for various options. Maternity nurses. Creche/nursery. Nanny: recruitment process including preparation, interviewing and selection. Mother's help. Child minder. Au pair. Reviewing childcare arrangements. Employer's and colleagues' perspectives. Sample contracts.

Chapter 3 Making the Most of Your Time Away from Work, p.99

Looking after yourself before and after the birth. Your emotional wellbeing. Your relationships. Practical ideas for before and after the birth. Helping older children cope. Making the decision to return to work. Employer's perspective. Preparing to return to work. Handling things people might say.

Chapter 4 Returning to Work, p.129

Managing your feelings. Practical tips. Looking after yourself. Thoughts to help you through the working day. Some ideas for helping you if your work involves travel. Employer's perspective. Children's perspective. Even more child care tips.

Chapter 5 Working from Home, p.163

Advantages and disadvantages of working from home. Preparation. Tips for making it work. Being assertive. Employer's perspective. Looking after yourself. Being self-employed. Sharing your workspace and home. Tools and technology. Children's perspective. Even more child care tips.

Chapter 6 Managing Yourself and Your Home, p.187

Managing yourself. Managing yourself at work. Paperwork. Housework tips. Paying others for cleaning and gardening. Shopping. Involving children. Preventing and reducing stress. Feeding the family.

Chapter 7 Building Children's Self Esteem and Independence, p.229

Building self-esteem. Communication. Developing emotional intelligence. Building personal independence. Potty training. Finance. Teenagers.

Chapter 8 Being Involved in Your Child's Education, p.269

Choosing pre-school education. Choosing a school. Evaluating a primary school. Helping your child prepare physically, psychologically and intellectually. Helping them through the first few months. Staying involved. Helping children become good learners. Homework or home learning. Parent/teacher consultations. Schools and finance.

Chapter 9 Making the Most of Family Traditions and Holidays, p.309

Building family relationships. Family meals. Bedtimes. Photographs. Birthdays. Christmas. Other seasonal ideas. Family holidays. Children's perspective. Yet more child care tips.

Mums the Word, p.333

To conclude.

Appendix A When Things Go Wrong, p.337

A solution focused approach to some of the difficulties that might arise under each of our chapter headings.

Appendix B Lists, Lists and More, p.359

Essential contacts. Essential dates. Christmas gifts. Birthdays. Photocopiable pages for evaluating a primary school. Packing lists. Weekly planner. Sample contract for an au pair.

Appendix C Bibliography, p.381

Recommended reading for each chapter heading.

Appendix D Websites, p. 387

Recommended sites for pregnancy, childcare, returning to work, family life and general support.

Appendix E Setting up a Support Group, p. 391

The story behind the support group we belonged to which was set up in 1981 together with the wide range of topics discussed throughout 27 years. Our simple formula for running the group.

Appendix F Easy Family Meals, p. 405

17 favourite tried and tested recipes.

Appendix G Helping Others, p. 415

Supporting new parents. Being a supportive partner.

Spinning Plates

Acknowledgements

Our love and thanks go to:

Our husbands, Graham and Neil, for supporting us throughout our journey as working mothers.

Our wonderful children - Simon, Alastair, AJ, Edward and Jessica - who make us the mothers we are.

Our parents, for their unconditional love.

Wendy's sister Sharon and Penny's cousin Jennifer for all their guidance and love.

To those who took care of our children while we worked and all our women friends - especially those in the Working Mums and Parentlink groups - who supported and encouraged us, when we were spinning our own plates.

Introduction

Why did we write this book?

For nearly 30 years we have benefited from the company of women who helped us through all that goes with being mothers and having paid work. We wanted to share our good fortune of the wisdom accumulated throughout those years with others in similar positions and help those engaged in this juggling act. We also care passionately about children having the best childhood possible so they can grow into confident, independent adults and feel the security and love of a family unit, whatever the context.

"..most women now work outside the home and have careers, as well as being mothers. In Britain 70 per cent of mothers of 9 to 12-month-old babies now do some paid work. This compares with only 25 per cent twenty-five years ago — a massive change in our way of life (Gregg et al 2005). Meantime, the children are cared for by someone other than their parents."

A Good Childhood by Richard Layard & Judy Dunn 2009

We know it's tough, because we've been working mothers since our first children were born, but we also know there are lots of things that can help. As we have written this from our personal experiences we chose to focus on working mothers. However, we acknowledge the significant role of working fathers and we believe many of the tips will be useful to them too. By offering some practical ideas for working parents, we hope life will be a little easier for all concerned so that the joy of a balanced life might be appreciated and positively embraced.

A guilt-free zone!

While working on the book, we noticed a recurrent theme was the guilt women feel when combining parenting and working, suspecting they don't actually do either job well enough. We believe it's time to let go of this guilt.

What does it cover?

Everything from working while you're pregnant, through to being involved in your child's education and their growing independence within the family unit. As well as lots of tried and tested 'secrets', tips and hints, there is guidance, humour and an offering of differing perspectives aimed at posing and answering the question, "have you thought.....?" Essentially it is a book full of practical ideas. It also explores the impact being a working parent has on some of the deeper issues of relationships, confidence and decision making. Because we know so many others are involved in ensuring you spin those plates successfully, we have added the perspectives of children, those who will be caring for them while you are at work and those of your employer. There are also personal stories from, and interviews with, some of the women we have come across, who have been kind enough to share their journeys with us. Because things can and do go wrong, our first appendix covers some issues that may arise, together with ideas for tackling them. To save you time, we provide you with a range of useful documents. You will find some of these within the chapters and others in Appendix B. We even give you a few choice responses to some of the things people might say to you as you embark on your balancing act!

The Law

We've included a few pieces of advice on the law. Of course the law changes faster than we can change this book, so it is important to check out the websites we suggest or the appropriate advice agencies.

How is it set out?

Because we know just how busy you are, we have structured the book so that it is easily accessible with lists of tips and hints under clear headings. The book can be dipped into whenever you need that little bit of help and over many years.

Grammar

We refer a lot to people in the singular, e.g. child, nanny, au pair and we have to identify them with pronouns. That has brought us up against the well known problem of using "he" or "she", "him" or "her", when the person may be male or female. To avoid that very cumbersome language, we've adopted "they" and "them". We know it's mixing singulars and plurals and could upset purists but it is increasingly accepted.

Who are we?

In 1982 Penny Clayton established a working mothers' support group of which Wendy Reus has been an active member since the birth of her first son in 1989. Having spent the years since, negotiating the minefield of motherhood while maintaining successful and varied careers: Penny as a Headteacher, Educational Consultant and Life Coach, who has had several articles published; Wendy as a personnel executive, trainer, recruitment consultant and business coach with blue chip companies and in children's television.

We acknowledge that we have written this book from very personal perspectives; we are both married, with supportive husbands and have five children between us. Despite writing from, what some may see as a privileged position, we have at times felt lost, scared and very unsure with all that motherhood and working can bring. We often thought about what we miss from not having extended families near to us. We didn't always get it right and wish we had access to this book ourselves at the time, because we think we would have been able to spin our plates so much better. We want this book to provide a supportive and inspirational resource for other mothers around the world who do not see childbirth as an end to their working lives. We offer hundreds of ideas, some seemingly contradictory, realising that you will want to pick and choose those that suit you, suit your job, your home and your pocket. We fervently hope this book will be like a wonderful wise affirming friend for you to call on.

Spinning Plates

Chapter One

Being Pregnant and Working

"Pregnancy is incredible. I can't believe you can create a human being just from the things you have around the house". Shang

So this is it. There's a plus sign on the testing wand, a doctor is handing you leaflets and pretty soon people are going to be expecting you to glow in some ill-defined yet apparently visible way. You are pregnant and life is about to change.

Suddenly everyone is eager to tell you about how your body won't feel like it belongs to you anymore, about how your brain will shortly be turned into an indistinct mush, about how much more difficult it will be for you to work. They'll tell you about all the joy and fulfilment you're about to experience as well as all the fear and uncertainty and, in the middle of it all, you would be forgiven for wondering how you will possibly be able to cope.

But, however you feel now and whatever people say, being pregnant while working doesn't need to be impossible. This chapter is intended to help you cope with the changes you'll face so that you can enjoy this defining, unsettling and thrillingly unique time in your life.

The World of Work

15 tips for working when pregnant
1
When should you tell your employer? We suggest you leave it until at least twelve weeks into the pregnancy and before the bump starts to show.

Personal Story.

"When I was pregnant with my son in 1989, I applied for a job of principal lecturer in a college. Unfortunately by the time they responded to my application and invited me in for interview, three months had gone by and I was now in the ninth month of my pregnancy. Ever the 'professional' (i.e. still very stupid), I turned up. The job was in the Faculty of Printing and Packaging (shortly to include publishing) so that meant 62 men (of the most traditional kind) and three very long suffering women on the staff. As I was shown round the college, it became apparent that the four men on the interviewing panel and every person we passed on the tour were all completely terrified that I was going to give birth there and then. Finally, the Dean (my boss- to- be) cracked and asked: 'how will you manage to hold down this job and look after your baby?' This was an unacceptable question in 1989 and the formidable 'woman from HR' blanched and reminded the Dean of this fact in no uncertain terms. He remained unfazed and I realised that if I wanted the job, I needed to answer his question satisfactorily. With HR person tutting in the background, I gave him a detailed account of the day in the life of a nanny until his eyes glazed over and I reckoned I was safe.

Anyway, I did not have the baby at the interview and no doubt out of sheer relief (and fear on the part of HR that I might report this 'unacceptable' line of questioning), I got the job!"

Wendy Boatman

2

At the time we wrote this women had the legal right to 26 weeks of "Ordinary Maternity Leave" and 26 weeks "Additional Maternity Leave". This is not dependent upon your length of employment but you do need to meet notification requirements. You get pay for the first 18 weeks – part of that at half pay. This is the legal minimum that you are entitled to, but you may find your employer will offer a far more generous scheme. At the end of your agreed maternity leave you must give eight weeks notice if you want to change the date of return. (Check with www.direct.gov for up to date information on rights and guidance.)

3

There are many good books and websites that will give you far more detailed information about your maternity rights than we plan to cover here. Do investigate what is available to you and then consider which option would suit you best. For example, when returning to work you have the right to ask to work flexibly if you have at least 26 weeks of qualifying service at the time the application is made. So research, and then think about your ideal work patterns. A big difficulty you might face is that you may want to get yourself organised to go back to work but don't know at this stage how you will feel once the baby is born. How can you organise child care if you don't know if you want to go back full or part time, or whether or not your employer will be able to accommodate that change? Have a chat with your employer and, without committing at this stage, consider your likely course of action. It can always be altered.

4

A simple request could make all the difference to managing at work- be bold! A friend of ours, in the later stages of her pregnancy, felt unable to make the commute during a particularly difficult week and asked whether her organisation would pay for her to stay in a hotel near her place of work. They were more than happy to oblige.

5

Some adjustments at work might be needed so do get help and support from a trusted colleague.

6

You may feel sick at roughly the same time each day so try to avoid key meetings at these times.

7

As your pregnancy continues it may be that you find yourself rather more distracted than usual with your brain resembling the fabled 'mush'. This is quite common and is one of the ways in which your body prioritises as it prepares for the new life growing inside you. Writing more lists than usual can help as well as other memory devices. A favourite mantra of ours is, "Don't be afraid to ask others for help!"

8

Consider scheduling medical appointments all on one day rather than breaking them up over several. Ask if any of these appointments could be during the evening – again, be bold! It may help to visit the hospital in person to organise this, as phoning all the different departments can sometimes prove difficult.

9

You may have to manage some politics at work. Be prepared for comments that sound insensitive such as. "You won't be here to see the project in June". People might see themselves as simply stating facts with no intention of excluding you. Learn to give up some control and watch out for being over-sensitive if you start to feel you're being ignored.

10

Trust that your colleagues will be able to carry on your work without you – after all, it's a great accolade that you can delegate and encourage responsibility in others. Why not treat your maternity leave as a sabbatical?

11

Assess where you work for safety and comfort. Your employer should arrange a risk assessment for you. If you are office based, find some way of putting your feet up under the desk and use a cushion for extra back support.

12

Take gentle walks as regularly as you can. Your lunch hour is ideal for a walk and for some fresh air.

13

What should you wear before the bump shows? Separates work well with longer tops. Good use of accessories like long scarves or necklaces can deflect attention from your disappearing waist. Choose a few comfortable, elegant pieces to make you feel great.

14

And once the bump shows? Accept and enjoy your new shape. Pretty underwear can help. By selecting forgiving shapes you may be able to limit the maternity clothes you need. Hiding under a sack or baggy clothes is not necessary. Wearing blocks of colour for work clothes looks good too (See Appendix D for websites on maternity clothes stockists' web-sites – good for working outfits too).

15

Remember, walk tall and celebrate your bump!

Personal Story

I commuted for eight months of my first and second pregnancies and encountered great kindness as well as sheer rudeness when it came to being offered a seat on a crowded train. When I had my large bump it was the summer months and a hot and crowded train was uncomfortable — even if you weren't pregnant. I did find that people were more likely to offer me their seat if I caught their eye and showed them my "Oh, I might be sick....possibly on your head" look! Miraculously they moved.... Wendy

"You should never say anything to a woman that even remotely suggests that you think she's pregnant unless you can see an actual baby emerging from her at that moment"

Things That It Took Me 50 Years to Learn, Dave Barry

Employer's Perspective

For all the changes pregnancy may bring to you, don't forget the challenges your employer will be facing too. It may be wonderful news for you, and your employer may also be genuinely delighted, but the impact for an organisation, of whatever size, cannot be underestimated. The following 5 points can help both parties.

1

Acknowledge the possible disruption that your absence from work will bring. You have rights and your employer will know them or will find out about them. Don't assume that you will have to fight your employer. Show empathy for their situation.

2

Explain your situation and likely plans as soon as you can, with the proviso that things may change. Employers appreciate having as much notice as possible.

3

You are more likely to have your needs met if you keep your employer informed of anything that may affect them.

4

Appreciate the impact of your pregnancy on your work and on your colleagues. Be helpful by trying to plan around this with issues such as medical appointments, work restrictions and sickness.

5

Are there things you could do to help cover your absence such as bringing your notes up to date, training the person who will cover your maternity leave, considering what will need to be done during your absence and even how this can be managed?

Spinning Yarns

Q: Should I have a baby after 35?

A: No, 35 children is enough.

Q: What is the most reliable method of determining a baby's sex?

A: Childbirth

Q: I'm two months pregnant now. When will my baby move?

A: With any luck, right after he finishes college.

Q: Is there anything I should avoid while recovering from childbirth?

A: Yes, pregnancy.

Q: My childbirth instructor says it's not pain I'll feel during labour, but pressure. Is she right?

A: Yes, in the same way that a tornado might be called an air current.

Q: When is the best time to get an epidural?

A: Right after you find out you're pregnant.

http://lifepassages.net/jokes.html

Wellbeing

13 ways to look after yourself

1

Pregnancy is *not* an illness, though you may be ill sometimes.

2

Just think, you no longer have to breathe in!

3

Understand that complete strangers may want to come up to you and stroke your tummy.

4

Enjoy your new shape, even the bigger boobs.

5

Specialist maternity clothes won't be essential. Hunt around for loose fitting garments making sure you feel comfortable and supported.

6

Get proper maternity bras and swimsuits.

7

Perhaps it's time to put the 7" heels away!

8

Doctors recommend carrying on as normal when pregnant. This can be misleading. Consider whether your "normal" is entirely appropriate during pregnancy.

9

Prepare for sickness and make allowances for yourself if you need to. Maybe keep a sick bag in the car, or can you try to be sick before you leave for work? Travel sickness wrist bands can help, as can ginger biscuits -eating them, not wearing them!

10

Eat little and often to minimize sickness. Keep a stash of food handy such as at your desk at work or in your bag or car. Drink plenty of water and listen to your body – cravings often serve a purpose!

11

Having a baby does not necessarily mean getting fat. A sensible diet and some exercise should help. Take time to rest and make time for yourself when possible.

12

Yoga, aqua-natal classes or other forms of relaxation can help. Both the NHS and the National Child Birth Trust (NCT – see Appendix D) will have information on antenatal classes.

13

Pregnancy will not necessarily prevent you from doing what you want in spite of the physical changes. Paula Radcliffe was aware of the changes pregnancy brought to her body and the implications for her marathon running. She adjusted and still ran.

Personal Story

One thing that I definitely did when I was at work when pregnant was ensure I always had food and water available — travelling a lot I couldn't afford to get caught short with no snacks. Don't be shy in a meeting getting out a banana and bottle of water! Better that than fainting on everyone! Eating little and often is a common thing I've realized with pregnant women.

Anonymous

Personal Story

I suffered an early miscarriage while I was at work. I didn't tell anyone but left the office early, got on the train and went to my doctors. I went back into work the following day and still didn't tell anyone. I mention this not because I am proud of my "just get on with it" attitude. Actually, I was so caught up in worrying about how it would be perceived if my bosses knew that I was even thinking of becoming pregnant (I might not get the promotion I had been waiting for) that I lost sight of my emotional and physical needs. Looking back, I may still have chosen not to share the information at work, but I could at least have given myself some time off to recover and deal with my loss.

Wendy

8 tips for looking after your emotional needs

1

If you are pregnant, whether planned or not, you can now choose to enjoy your pregnancy. How you respond to your condition may determine how you feel throughout and, while it might not make the pregnancy easier, it might make it more fun.

2

Pregnancy *will* come to an end and relatively soon, to the envy of most elephants, so don't wish the time away.

3

Having concerns about being a good mother is perfectly natural. It is also common to worry about not having maternal feelings, especially when you are so used to being in control of your life. Many new mothers say these worries disappear once the baby arrives.

Spinning yarns

Q: *My wife is five months pregnant and so moody that sometimes she's borderline irrational.*
A: *So what's your question?*

http://lifepassages.net/jokes.html

4

Don't forget our mantra, "Ask for what you need of yourself and others." Pregnancy is a time to pay attention to your emotional and physical demands and do something about them.

Personal Story

"I think one thing from my experience is to try not to be a martyr or a hero — the baby comes first and if you can't do something don't be afraid to say no and put your health first. I spent time worrying about feeling guilty for not attending meetings or doing something which was not good for baby or me and, in the end, everyone was fine about it and understanding. Talk about things - don't let them build up as your emotions are all over the place and you can feel quite vulnerable and emotionally irrational!"

Anonymous

"I began changing when I was pregnant with Vanessa. I had been wanting that child so much, for so long. Don't forget I was 30. And something happened to me while that baby was growing inside me. I began feeling a unity with people, to understand that we do not give life to a human being to have it killed by B-52 bombs or have it jailed by Fascists or destroyed by social injustice. I began to love people and become involved with causes."

Jane Fonda from "A Celebration of Babies" edited by Sally Emerson.

5

Everyone, but everyone, will have an opinion about what to do, or not to do, about being pregnant and having a baby. Listen to them all! There can be real gems of advice. Then decide what works for you, your baby and your partner.

6

Miscarriages can happen so you may wish to announce your news at a point when you feel your pregnancy is more secure.

7

People will react differently to your news. Some will be very pleased for you, some jealous, some will assume you won't return to work, others will be over protective. So clarifying your own thoughts about your news will enable you to respond to all comers. What you decide is your business of course. You can make life easier for yourself, for instance you could make it clear that you are delighted and intend to return to work if all is well.

8

Find a confidante, maybe a work colleague, with whom you can chat freely about your experiences during pregnancy.

Relationships

6 hints for keeping them healthy

1

Involve your partner in the changes you're noticing; share thoughts on him being there at the birth; discuss financial implications of maternity leave, returning to work or staying at home, while acknowledging you may change your mind.

2

Investigate support groups (see Appendix E "Setting Up a Support Group") – linking in with mothers, not just pregnant women. See also Appendix D for useful networking web sites.

3

Spend as much quality time with your partner as possible. Go out and enjoy yourselves or just make time to be alone - you won't have as much time when the baby comes!

4

If possible, involve your partner in ante-natal classes. These can help the adjustment process, be a great source of information as well as great fun and a way of making new friends for you both.

5

Both new parents need some fuss and acknowledgement but having a bump often means that prospective mothers get their share and fathers don't. Involve and include the baby's father as early as possible.

6

If you plan to return to work and know who will be looking after your child already, think about how you will build the relationship.

Personal Story

Having joined an ante-natal group, Neil and I had spent most of the five evening classes in giggles. For instance, he got the prize for falling asleep at a record rate in the relaxation class — that would have been an achievement except he was supposed to be learning how to help me relax during labour! On the last session we switched from theory into practice and had a real live baby brought into the class so that the (very experienced) parents could show us how to bath a baby. Well, they left and we then went on to talk about breast feeding. The health visitor asked us "who is going to try breast feeding"? About half the mums put their hands up, including the woman to my right. Her partner was aghast. "What do you mean you are going to give it a go? "Well", she said quite defensively, "I thought I would at least try." "Ok", he said (obviously still in practical demonstration mode) "but which one of us men is going to be the baby?!"

Wendy

Practical

9 tips to make life easier

1

Research your local hospitals – talk to recent Mums but still make your own decision.

2

It's always good to have a birth plan but don't be too tied to it. Be flexible and open-minded.

3

Consider the financial implications of not working or of taking time off work for a period of time. It may be necessary to save money during pregnancy to cover your bills while you're on maternity leave.

4

It's a good idea to complete any outstanding DIY tasks in the house before maternity leave, such as fixing the leaking tap, buying a new washing machine or preparing for where your baby will sleep. The more you can do before the baby arrives the better you will feel.

5

Save maternity leave (assuming you will have some!) for personal preparation, recovery and time with the baby (see Chapter 3).

6

Fill the freezer ready for when the baby arrives so you don't have to worry about cooking in those first few weeks.

Personal Story

Have your midwife's phone number in your mobile so you can call her with questions to stop those panicky thoughts developing in your mind. I had a few days when I couldn't feel the baby move and I called her and she was great and reassured me then organised for me to go to the hospital to be monitored.

Anonymous

7

If possible, it is worth trying to schedule your midwife appointments with the same person.

8

Whatever your pastimes, this is a good time to enjoy them, such as reading, going to the cinema, theatre or going for long walks. Once the baby is born it will be difficult to do these things for a time.

9

It's probably not a good idea to have any major hairstyle changes at this point as your face may change shape temporarily as a result of pregnancy.

Child's perspective

9 ideas to help children adapt to the changes

1

If there are older children in your family choose the time and the words carefully when telling them about your pregnancy. Be prepared for a wide variety of reactions; from pleasure to anger or even complete indifference – these emotions may change over time.

2

It may be helpful to start with - "I/we have some news.....we are having a baby" and then give them space to absorb this news and ask questions then or later.

3

Children usually ask specific questions they want answers to, so additional information may not be necessary, such as some of the gory details of pregnancy and birth. However, do encourage them to ask questions and voice any concerns they may have.

4

What you should tell children and when is very age-dependent and influenced by their individual personalities. For example, a teenager is likely to be concerned about the impact on them and how their family appears to the outside world, whereas a much younger child might only be interested in whether their mother will change. Some are anxious about the gender of the baby or they are wondering whether they will want to play with them in the future.

5

Avoid saying, "Isn't it exciting...you will have a new brother/sister?" as this was a choice made without their involvement.

6

Older children can be anxious about their mother's physical tiredness, especially after a day's work, and can even suspect the expected baby might be personally to blame. Do explain that tiredness and an increased number of medical appointments are all quite normal.

7

Some older children worry about reduced family income, of a possible change in child-care arrangements and of being "replaced" by the expected baby while they attend nursery or school. You can help allay any fears by talking about these issues and by being sensitive about any changes.

8

Part of the preparation process which could affect your older child may include changes to the house. Do include them, especially if they have a degree of choice and involvement. Wendy had options about which room could be used for a nursery when her third child came along which gave the older two a chance to decide if they wanted to switch rooms. This was all quite exciting for them and they then chose to help set up the nursery.

9

Think about arrangements for the care of other children for when you go into labour. Is there a neighbour or close family member who is prepared to come in and look after them while you go into hospital or the room where you are to have the baby if it is a home birth? Discuss your child care plans with your children as it will help them to be prepared and feel included in decisions being made.

Personal Story

Towards the end of 1983, a couple of years into my first headship of a small primary school and with an excellent deputy, it felt a good time to have a second child. Delighted to be pregnant, I felt it was time to confide in the deputy and asked if she could spare me a few minutes in the office. As soon as she heard my news she looked rather troubled, which was not quite the reaction I had expected.

Quietly she stood up, crossed the floor to the door, closed it firmly and turned to me saying, "So am I." We stared at each other for a few moments trying to take in the news and then sharing our predicted dates discovered they were incredibly close.

A few days later I went along to a heads' meeting and sought out the inspector attached to the school. I asked her for a word in private and explained our situation. She took in the news very quickly, then threw back her head, laughed and declared it was the nicest little problem she had ever had to deal with.

With her support the two pregnant leaders of this little school set about coping with our needs and those of the pupils and whole school community. Whose morning sickness was the least troublesome? Who felt well enough to take assembly? Which herbal tea seemed to work best? Did we want to share the purchase of a huge consignment of nappies for newborn babies, which could be delivered to the school? How should we respond to the male inspector who, when visiting the school, suggested we should plan more carefully in future?

As the summer term came to a close and we resembled Tweedle Dum and Tweedle Dee presenting end of year prizes at a whole school assembly, exhausted but positive, we handed over to an experienced deputy from another school and a senior colleague from our own and went home for about three weeks relaxation before the births.

The babies were born within five days of each other; we both took four months maternity leave, returning the following January. We found great comfort sharing our experiences with each other. An added bonus was a greater affinity with parents as we were now able to share the experiences of motherhood.

Penny

Spinning Plates

Chapter Two

Arranging Child Care

Child Care

Just as you're beginning to get used to being a parent and having a new member of the family, it seems in no time at all that you are expected to make decisions about who is to look after your baby when you return to work. We both found anticipating the separation to be quite painful and making the right decision about child care tough. Of course, if your child could choose, they might want someone akin to the advert placed by Jane and Michael Banks in the film, "Mary Poppins", i.e, "If you want this choice position, have a cheery disposition … you must be kind, you must be witty, very sweet and fairly pretty." You, of course, will have other considerations. How do you choose the right care for your child? How much can you afford to pay someone to look after your child? Is your home big enough to have someone live in your house? Are there factors at work to think about? What would suit you best? It can all seem very daunting. To help you, this chapter briefly covers the main options for childcare and raises some questions that you may wish to think about as you make plans. Your key options are likely to be:

> A crèche or nursery
>
> A nanny
>
> A mother's help
>
> A child minder
>
> An au pair
>
> Family/partner/friends

Our table sets out these options to help with your decision…

Childcare Options

Creche or Nursery

Advantages	*Employers may provide nursery vouchers to help with costs. *Social interaction with other children and carers. *Consistency of location and no staffing responsibilities. *No responsibility for tax and insurance. *Peace of mind as regulated and inspected. *It may be at your work-place. *Range of activities provided. *Children become used to a structured learning environment. *Your home is not disrupted!!
Disadvantages	*Cost may be too high. *Taking child out of home every morning. *Sick children unable to attend. *Location may prove difficult. *Relationships with carers more distant. *There may be a turnover of carers. *Less control over organisation and activities. *Caters for a restricted age group and may not accommodate siblings.
Further Considerations	*Cost is per child. *Length of waiting list. *Length of notice period required should your employment circumstances change. *No worries about the carer being ill as the crèche or nursery will manage this.

Childcare Options

Nanny

Advantages	*Child cared for in their own home — not having to get your child out in the morning.
	*Individual attention for the child.
	*Recruited with your values/concerns in mind.
	*Greater control over diet and discipline.
	*Can develop close relationships.
	*Can delegate many duties such as doctor's visits.
	*If your child is ill they are still taken care of.
	*Can negotiate hours to suit your working pattern.
	*Can look after all your children, which means keeping siblings together.
	*Can set your own agenda for activities.
	*If you have to move home, your nanny may be willing to move with you.
Disadvantages	*Cost.
	*Car may be needed.
	*Accommodation - if living in.
	*Turnover and disruption. Good nannies very often want to work with babies or at least to have their charges at home.
	*Lack of privacy.
	*Can put a strain on relationships.
	*Can feel responsible for them and become too involved.
	*Need to organise their salary, tax and N.I..

Childcare Options

Further Considerations	*Playgroups, coffee mornings, nanny networks etc., can all provide opportunities for children to socialise even with a carer in your home.
	*You need to feel comfortable about "managing" someone in your own home.
	*If the nanny is ill but lives in, they may still be able to look after your child.
	*If they live in you can leave them and your child in bed if you have an early start.
	*Live in nannies can cover trips away and nights out.
	*Can have nannies who live-in during the week only.
	*Consider nanny share with another family but note the nanny would then need to be registered as a child-minder.
	*Cost can be constant however many children are cared for..

Mother's Help

Considerations	*Similar to the nanny. However they may not be able to cover the number of hours you need, won't be as qualified and therefore are unable to take sole care for as many hours.
	*A less expensive alternative.
	*Wouldn't normally live in.

Childcare Options

Child Minder

Advantages	*Reasonable cost. *No invasion of your own home. *Children experience another family household. *Registration a legal requirement so homes and practice are regularly inspected. *Likely to mix with a small number of other children of varying ages. *Normally, no tax or insurance to deal with. *No provision necessary for a room, car and meals. *Can be a reassuring source of knowledge and support as they are often experienced parents. *May be able to accommodate an ill child.
Disadvantages	*Huge amount of organisation required to take your child and all their equipment to someone else's home every morning. *Time pressure in the mornings getting yourself and children ready. *Time pressure in the evenings to get back on time. *Less flexibility as child minders often have their own families. *May need to accommodate other children's needs, such as collection from school.
Further Considerations	*Cost per child. *The relationship is typically likely to be longer.

Childcare Options

Au Pair

Advantages	*Cost effective, can do 5 hours a day plus 2 nights babysitting. *Cultural and language enhancement for the family. *Prepared to clean. *Works well with school-age children. *If it doesn't work out, it is easy to dismiss them if you went through an agency.
Disadvantages	*Untrained. *Need to adjust to leaving home. *May become another responsibility. *Restricted language. *Unsuitable for younger children. *Unlikely to be able to drive. *Will need to study. *There at week ends. *Accommodation essential. *Lack of privacy. *Very often you are taking an au pair purely on trust as you may not have been able to see them or even speak to them prior to their engagement.
Further considerations	*Au pair share is possible. *They can augment their salary cleaning/babysitting. *Can get returning au pair to find her own replacement Wendy's au pairs interviewed prospective candidates on the telephone and helped with their training. *Agencies often don't see the au pairs themselves. *May want to be part of the family.

Childcare Options

Family/Partner/Friends

Advantages	*Close relationships are built. *Cost effective. *Familiar surroundings. *Trust.
Disadvantages	*Can put a strain on relationships. *Harder to dictate your requirements.
Further Considerations	*What happens if it goes wrong? *Need clarity of roles at the outset and regular reviews.

Before and After School Clubs

Advantages	*An extension of the school day. *Familiar surroundings and other children. *Breakfast clubs can prevent children being rushed in the mornings and gently introduced to the school day. *Homework can be completed at school with help sometimes available. *Relatively low cost.
Disadvantages	*Timings may not be flexible enough. *Child may feel they have few hours to relax at home.
Further Consideration	Some children may find the extended day very tiring.

Maternity Nurses

Maternity Nurses are trained nurses or nannies who specialise in the care of newborn babies. Their duties would normally include supporting the mother for the first 4-8 weeks of the baby's life, but can be for longer. The purpose is to help the family with routine in those early weeks and can enable the parents to establish a pattern. As the maternity nurses are experienced they can be a great source of advice and guidance for new parents and will willingly take care of all aspects of baby care. An advantage is that most will take care of night feeds, either bottle-feeding or bringing the baby to you if breast-feeding. They will often sleep in the baby's room. This is, naturally, a costly option!

It may be that someone you already know could look after your child. This happened to Penny and a friend of ours.. . . .

Personal Stories: Someone You Know

Being pregnant for the first time and working as a deputy head in a primary school I had plenty of opportunities to consider other people's children and wonder how mine would turn out. There was one girl in my class who seemed perfect in every way - bright, thoughtful, courteous and so mature.

While teaching her one day, it occurred to me that her parents must have done a pretty good job and maybe they could do the same for my child.

I knew her mother, Maureen, had a job as a dinner lady in a local school and understood she might like a change, so I asked her daughter to suggest that she might become my childminder once the baby was born.

So began a long and happy association with this family. We needed to organise her registration as a childminder, to arrange opportunities for us to get to know her and to plan for the care to begin. One thing that worked really well was that Maureen was only the third person to hold our babies - after us as parents. In this way we felt she could also bond with them. Maureen MacDonald didn't have children from other families to care for and our relationship was almost that of an extended family. It worked a treat and I will always be grateful to her for being there advising me as well as providing such excellent care for my children over a ten-year period.

Penny

A friend of Wendy's, Karen, while on holiday in France, was chatting to a local girl who was a waitress at one of their favourite restaurants. Over the next few days they got to know one another better and it led to her moving to England and becoming her children's au pair.

Crèche/Nursery

In most areas of this country there is a crèche or nursery, operated either by Social Services or run privately, which will care for children for the whole of the typical working day. Additionally, many organisations provide work-place nurseries. They cater for babies and children up to school age and provide food and sleeping arrangements, as well as toys and activities to help with their development. It is wise to visit and make enquiries before making your decision as they can vary in quality. A disadvantage of this form of childcare is that, if children are ill, the nursery may refuse to look after them until they are better. It's a good idea to have a backup plan.

Spinning yarn

Police were called to a nursery where a three-year-old was "resisting a rest".

http://www.clevermag.com/humor/humorarchIII.htm

Choosing a nursery:
3 ideas to help you make the decision

1

Visit four or five different nurseries, even if you have a recommendation. This way you will be able to make some comparisons and get a feel for the one that is right for you and your family.

2

Location, ease of access, transport, parking and fees are all important considerations but your gut feeling can be even more important.

3

You may wish to read any Ofsted (Office of Standards in Education) reports on your selected nurseries. Try an Internet search! Do remember these are often only valid on the day of the inspectors' visit. Be aware of any unsatisfactory comments in these reports but make sure to check the date of the inspection. Also find out about any gaps in service mentioned in the report and whether something has been done to improve things. You may find that issues identified in the report have already been speedily resolved resulting in a much-improved service.

25 things to consider

1

There are specific legal requirements for ratios of adults to children that vary according to the child's age.

When we wrote this, they were:

under 2 years - 1:3

2 – 3 years - 1:4

over 3 years - 1:8

2

Anyone working in the nursery should be familiar with these figures. If staff are absent, a temporary member of staff or agency worker will need to be recruited and, until they arrive, there may be a poorer ratio. This will be fine for a short while but do ask about the contingency plans for staff absence.

3

Find out about qualifications. When we wrote this, all staff must have enhanced Criminal Records Bureau (CRB) checks so feel free to ask about this. To work with such young children, holding the appropriate NVQ level 2 is the minimum requirement but NVQ 3 is standard. Over 50% of staff must be suitably qualified.

4

Just so that you are aware, male nursery nurses can change nappies.

5

Ask about staff turnover. It may be an indicator of low staff morale or there may be more acceptable reasons.

6

Ask whether there is a key worker system in place. If there is, the key worker is the main carer for a number of children and handles all aspects such as observations and assessments. This does not mean others won't have a relationship with all the children.

7

Check how many of the staff are first-aid trained. Ideally there should be one in each area, someone on duty at the opening and closing of the day, as well as a substitute if any of the others are on holiday. Special paediatric first aid training is essential.

8

Find out what contingency plans are in place for tackling illness and emergencies. Is there a handbook for parents in which all the policies are set out? It will be necessary to have contact details for both parents as well as an extra emergency contact. It is also likely you will be asked to provide additional items to aid security such as a photo with a name and password for anyone else who might be sent to pick your child up. Alternatively, you may well be telephoned to check if it's OK to release your child to someone other than the parents. You should find this reassuring rather than an irritant.

9

Babies should be allowed to follow their own sleeping patterns in line with your preferences. You might like to check their policy so your baby can sleep according to your wishes.

10

Ask how the nursery manages allergies. There should be a procedure in place with a care plan and a risk assessment. Some staff should have been trained in giving medication and administering an EpiPen. Ask about checking for "use-by" dates on medication.

11

A nursery should be able to accommodate children with disabilities and should have a SENCO (Special Educational Needs Coordinator) based in the nursery with further support at a regional level. These people set individual plans for children with special needs and regularly meet with parents to track and review progress. If physical access is an issue and the nursery is upstairs, check there is a lift. There may be children with severe disabilities in the nursery. Find out how they are integrated and managed and, if you see that the nursery successfully accommodates a wide range of needs, then this may well prove to be a warm and enriching environment for your child.

12

Notice the cleanliness of the rooms, furnishings and equipment. Check whether gloves and aprons are worn when the staff are feeding and changing nappies. Are you happy about the cleaning and sterilisation routines?

13

What do you notice about the atmosphere? Do the activities seem interesting? Are a variety of materials being used? Is there an opportunity for exploratory play? Is the outdoor area used and seen as an extension of the inside room with tools, toys and wellies for splashing in puddles? Is there evidence of children using technology, cameras and computers? Are the themes for activities carefully selected such as those linked with what is happening in the local community, rather than obvious topics like the weather? If work is displayed on the walls, has it been done by children? Do the children appear engrossed in what they are doing? Are there pre-writing activities such as finger-painting and sand shapes? Is it OK for the children to be messy?

14

Check whether cultural differences are catered for. Are children allowed to use their hands to eat rather than only cutlery? Are kosher and halal foods available?

15

Find out how religious festivals are handled. Are they acknowledged? Are they celebrated? Look around the room to see whether there is a variety of stimulus for social play such as woks, diverse foodstuffs and saris rather than just token pictures on the walls.

16

Take a look at the selection of books. Do they represent the diversity of society? Are parents from different countries made to feel welcome? Can anyone speak a few words in the languages currently spoken by the families of children in the nursery?

17

If children run up to you when you visit, it may be an indication that they are bored so be aware and check out any concerns you might have. Do the staff appear interested in you, your child, the children in the nursery and their job in general?

18

How well are parents informed about the educational provision on offer? We know of one nursery that lets parents experience for themselves the six early learning goals specified by the last Government for very young children. This included tasting glue, playing in the sand, and moving on all fours!

19

If you are a single parent, you may wish to ask how the nursery manages tricky subjects like father's day and mother's day. A simple way round this is to let children join in making cards addressed 'To someone special'.

20

Find out what kinds of records are kept on the children and ask what you will be able to see. They will range from photographs, daily feedback sheets to formal records of activities undertaken. Records will include progress made in areas such as language development and the acquisition of fine and large motor skills. Daily observation sheets will help staff plan the activities for the coming days.

21

Some nurseries offer trial sessions for free. This may be a very good option as you will discover how everything works in practice and how quickly happy relationships are formed.

22

If you know your busiest times at work during the year, check if the nursery is able to help you by increasing the hours on a temporary basis. If your busiest times are around public holidays, such as Christmas, check if the nursery will be open. If not, you will need to arrange back-up care in advance.

23

Most nurseries encourage parents to stay for a short time and gradually extend the time the child is left with them. Could you do this?

24

Discover how the nursery manages health issues. Every illness has an incubation period. Fact sheets should be available in the nursery. You may be notified if your child is under the weather, if he or she has a fall or sustains an injury. You should always be informed if your child has a bump to the head and told what signs of concussion to look out for. You can expect a member of staff to go with your child to hospital and then hand over to a parent as soon as possible. Unfortunately it is not the nursery's problem if parents have no alternative care arrangements.

25

Ask how the nursery deals with behaviour issues.

Aide memoire for visiting nurseries prior to selection
Do your research.
Trust your instincts.
Adult: child ratios. Legal requirements met, plus provision of individual attention?
Qualified staff?
Cleanliness, hygiene and safety?
Atmosphere. Does it look fun? Wide range of activities?
Communication re the educational provision.
Sensitivity to your needs (cultural, first baby, single parent etc.).
Behaviour management?
Kinds of records and access to them?
Trial session?
Pace the induction phase gradually?
Check what happens if your child is ill.

Nanny

This is a person who has had formal training in child care and holds a relevant certificate such as the NNEB (Nursery Nurses Examination Board). A nanny will perform all household duties relating to the children in his or her care but is not expected to carry out cleaning, laundry or any tasks relating to other family members. The employer must make tax and national insurance payments for them.

Wendy learned the hard way through mistakenly paying tax for one nanny who hadn't paid enough tax from her previous employment. Ensure that you are working out tax payments based on the basic rate of tax.

There are specialist companies who can do all this for you e.g. www.nannytax.co.uk.

Having a nanny can be an expensive option and you may need to be able to provide appropriate accommodation In addition, there can be hidden costs like food or maybe a car. On the positive side a nanny is trained, children can remain in their own home environment and you won't need to do quite so much before you leave for work each morning.

Wendy had a Monday to Friday nanny, which she thought worked really well as there was cover during the week, but at the weekends the nanny went home so the family had their space and privacy. There are some nannies that will work in your home on a daily basis only and, therefore, don't need you to provide accommodation.

Nanny Recruitment Process

Preparation – 5 tips

1

Decide what you want from childcare. What would work best for the age of your child? What suits your house, your lifestyle, where you work, your budget and your hours? Having a nanny when you live in a remote country area may not work if they feel isolated - a child minder may work better. If you travel a lot with your work you may need live-in support.

2

Do include your partner and, if appropriate, older children when thinking through your options.

3

Find out what's available in your area. A well-established nanny network may be able to help find someone who is looking for a new job. Talk to your health visitor, your neighbours, other mums and babysitters.

4

Consider different ways of recruiting such as word of mouth, advertising, magazines such as The Lady, post office notice boards, agencies, and the internet. You can use more than one.

5

Whether nanny or childminder, make sure a job description is available. It is important to be clear from the start about what you will need them to do. Include the routine aspects and the not-so-fun parts but don't overstress them. Think of any additional perks you could provide such as an early finish on Friday afternoons, the use of a car at weekends or during the working week. Perhaps you could offer an extra week's holiday?

Selection – 13 tips

1

Select your candidates from their letters and CV's. Try to find out if they have a real passion for working with children. If you are using an agency, they might help with this.

2

Prepare for the interview with some well thought out questions. See later in this chapter for some examples. Remember that your interviewee is likely to be nervous and this isn't a business interview. Help them to feel welcome and relaxed. Give the interview your full attention and let them meet your child/children. When Wendy's children were a bit older she used to get them to show the nanny their bedrooms, so that they had a bit of time together unobserved. The children very quickly felt warmth towards the nanny –

or not. Their opinions were always considered although they didn't ultimately make the decision.

3

It may help to see all the candidates on the same day so a decision can be made as quickly if possible.

4

Give the candidate time to ask any questions they might have.

5

Ask about references and take note of telephone numbers.

6

Show them an example of the children's weekly routine to give them a good idea of what they will be expected to do.

7

Show them their accommodation if they are going to be living in.

8

Is there something hands on that they could do during the interview? Feed the baby? Read to a child? Something that allows them to show their skill. A poor interviewee doesn't mean they will be a poor nanny - normal professional interviewing rules don't always apply here. Work out what really matters to you and look for that.

9

Once you have finished the interview, be clear about when you will let them know the result of the interview, the start date, their salary and holidays.

10

Choose your successful candidate. If you really don't feel any were suitable, then don't make an offer and re-advertise instead, perhaps using a different route. Don't be tempted to appoint just because you're desperate.

11

Let the other candidates know as soon as possible that they haven't been successful, giving them constructive feedback if they ask for it. Letting them know that you have chosen a candidate "who had even more skills and experience" than they did, can still leave them feeling good about themselves.

12

If you are lucky enough to have a choice of candidates then it may be prudent just to let the definite "noes'" know the result and wait to talk to your first choice before informing your second. Your first choice may refuse the job.

13

If your candidate says 'yes', let them know that it is a conditional offer dependent upon references. You may want to find out about what their previous responsibilities were, what the employer liked about them, what they would want them to improve, if they could. Check absence rates. Ask "Is there anything that you think it would be helpful for me to know?" Employers can be nervous about giving references that are critical in some way, but explain that it really is helpful for you to know. Sometimes, a reference might raise a criticism or concern that might not worry you at all such as, "She was always tidying up". What works in one household may not work in another. Trust your instincts.

Suggested questions when interviewing a nanny/carer

See the end of this chapter for a suggested interview outline and sample questions. Select from these and think about the kind of responses you are looking for.

Induction – 2 ideas

1

The amount of time you have available to introduce your nanny to the family will influence what preparations you need to make. Have a folder filled with important information such as instructions on how to use your domestic appliances, emergency contact details, lists of friends and neighbours, maps of the local area, your child's routine and playgroup hours. Some nannies need a lot of guidance and some are happy to be thrown in at the deep end. Preparing as much as you can and then trusting that they will cope is a good way to approach this.

2

Spend some time in the early days talking to the nanny. What is she enjoying? What is she finding difficult? What would improve things for her? How does your child feel? Talk to her as a trained professional by setting some time aside for feedback.

Review

If for any reason you feel unhappy, decide how serious it is. If you are concerned for the child's safety or happiness then don't waste any time in tackling this. Talk to your nanny sooner rather than later and give them a reasonable amount of time to improve before reviewing again. Be clear about the reasons for your concerns and have specific examples where possible. If the problem is so serious that you don't think it can be solved, in a reasonable time, or if earlier warnings haven't worked, then you may have to end the employment. In such a case, make your reasons clear in writing and pay the nanny's notice period.

Personal Story

I am able to reflect on many great success stories with our child care, live-in nannies, daily nannies, au-pairs, even my mother! There were also some not so successful stories and I share this one with you, not to worry you, but to illustrate that despite the fact things can go wrong there can be some positives. In this case my eldest learnt about aspects of people management and I learnt that, despite my concern that I always needed to "get it right", if the children have something significant in their life that is constant (parents, their school, each other) then they cope with the lumps and bumps along the way and it can be a very useful learning exercise — for all concerned!

The agency provided me with a girl from the Gran Canaries. We picked her up at the airport Thursday evening and I arranged to take Friday off to show her the ropes. Natalia (pretty young 19 year old) emerged at 5.00pm on the Friday saying that she was suffering from jet lag — I should have picked up the first sign at that point, I guess! On the Saturday we returned from the boys' football practice at lunchtime to find her sprawled on the sofa in her silk pyjamas talking on her mobile.

Her breakfast/brunch/lunch plates were stacked above the empty dishwasher. She continued to ignore us all. When she deigned to finish her call, her questions were all about the nearest night clubs and that she was planning to go out that evening.

I explained to her that I needed some help with our 3

children and that her role was to give me a hand. My son beckoned me into the other room and said he thought I was being rather hard on her! Despite getting a Spanish speaking friend to go through our expectations of her (e.g. unlike the Spanish we were not able to accommodate her eating at 9.00pm and starting work at lunch time the next day), she continued to view her time with us as free accommodation whilst she partied.

After 4 days my 14 year old said "If you don't get rid of her, I will!" The agency was very supportive and agreed that she should no longer stay with us. Explaining to her in my very poor Spanish and her limited English that she needed to go wasn't easy and, I'm sure as she realised what I was saying, her knowledge of English significantly reduced!

It turned out that her mother had suggested that she leave her home as she was partying so much and needed to "get a job", which was why she had come over. Shame her mother hadn't explained that in getting a job she would need to perform some duties to hold it!

Wendy

Nanny sharing

This is when two or more families share a nanny in one of their homes. This works best when families sharing live very close to each other and when relationships and communication between the parties are good. Issues such as holidays, standards and expectations, having other people's children in your home and the use of a car will need to be tackled. A check should be made with the household insurance policy that it is permissible to have other people's children cared for by a shared nanny.

Mother's Help

Usually this person has no formal training and, therefore, cannot be expected to fulfil the same functions as a nanny but will carry out more general household duties. They are to work alongside a parent, which can be great if the parent works from home. The salary would not be as high as for a trained nanny but the employer must still pay tax and national insurance.

Child Minder

This is often a woman who has school-age children of her own. They must be registered with Social Services and regularly inspected to ensure that their home is suitable and safe for young children.

8 things to consider

1

Visit two or three possible childminders.

2

Ideally choose someone who lives close to you or your work to minimise the journey. Will your partner be able to help with delivering and collecting?

3

Find out about the routines in place in the home. Is the childminder prepared to take your child to playgroups and so on if this is what you want?

4

Discuss what you feel about certain household rules but don't be overly concerned if there are differences. Children adapt very well. However, if the differences are more fundamental, such as approaches to discipline, check they are happy to do it your way or come to a compromise.

5

You may be able to have a trial period. It will be valuable to spend a little time at the childminder's house with your child during the settling in period.

6

Create some time for you and the childminder to develop your relationship.

7

Find out whether your child can still attend if he or she is sick. Have a back-up plan if the child isn't able to go or if your childminder falls ill.

8

If your childminder doesn't work in the holidays, it
may be possible to engage a second childminder.
Consider a student looking for holiday employment.

Au pair

This is usually a young person from another country
wishing to work in a family to improve their English.
There are certain requirements regarding their
employment and differences dependent on whether
they are from the EU or not. In general, au pairs are
not expected to work more than five hours per day
and may help with a range of household duties. Due to
language difficulties, they may require greater
supervision than a Mother's Help. Au pairs can work
well if you work from home or if children have started
school and you need cover for the hours between the
end of the school day and your return from work. Au
pairs are expected to study and you can normally find
local colleges who offer English language courses with
this in mind.

Personal Story

*I have had some great successes with au pairs and some real
disasters! What I found worked was having a good au pair,
who then found me the next girl to take over (girls in my
case, but there are male au pairs. I was keen to have a male
but interestingly my children weren't!). The current au pair
would choose friends that she knew would be right for the*

role and was able to explain to them what was required in their own language. The new au pair then did the same when it was her time to leave.

Wendy.

6 ideas for recruiting an au pair

1

It's particularly important when recruiting an au pair that you should be clear in your mind about what you want before you start the process. Remember you must avoid unlawful discrimination so be sure that you can justify your requirements. For example one of Wendy's sons was studying Spanish so for that reason she chose a Spanish speaking au pair. Ensure the candidates know your requirements before they are interviewed.

2

Agencies can be a good way of finding au pairs. Do, however, be aware that the agent may not have talked with au pair they are sending you. They should be able to provide you with a list of suitable candidates, guidance on what to expect, an example of a contract, network groups for the au pairs, references, recommended pay scales and follow-up support and advice for both parties.

3

Provide the candidates (and agency) with as much information beforehand about what you require and about the family, home, area and the facilities near by. You may need to know if they have any allergies/medical issues.

4

You may find you don't need to use an agency if you hear of a suitable candidate through other au pairs, through friends or even after a chance meeting on holiday.

5

When interviewing you may wish to select some of our questions, bearing in mind that the interviewees English could well be limited, you may be conducting the interview over the telephone, and that the role is different from that of a nanny. Ask only questions that relate to your justifiable requirements. Ensure that you have covered as much as possible of your requirements in the role description, before the conversation takes place. Examples might be that you are happy for them to study English whilst with you and that you need someone who is comfortable with pets in the home. Finding out what they know about the country and if they know anyone who lives here will help them manage their expectations and help them to settle.

6

When your au pair arrives, the norm is that he or she is responsible for covering the costs of getting to the UK but you collect them from, and return them to, the airport or station. Ask for a photograph to be sent to you before arrival to help you recognise the airport.

Note:

Au pairs and mother's helps differ from other child care providers in that their role is principally to help the household, rather than have sole care of the children. Their relationship with the children is, therefore, not as important. If they get on very well with the children then that is a bonus.

Agencies may not provide you with a contract to use. An example of a contract is set out at the end of this chapter.

4 more ideas

1

Au pairs will also appreciate a folder filled with useful information as outlined in the section on nannies.

2

If they have just arrived in the country they may need some time to adjust and recover from their journey before you go through too much information with them. Some of this can be covered gradually but it may be a good idea to go through your expectations of them in the first day or so.

3

As an au pair would normally only work five hours a day, you may need a different arrangement during school holidays. This could be time off in lieu/extra payment or you may need an additional form of childcare.

4

If the au pair is in the house and is free to keep an eye on one child, how about spending some individual time with the others?

Personal Story

When we went on our summer holiday our au pair chose not to return to her home for a visit so I suggested that she might like to bring her Slovak family over to England and stay at our house. They had a great time visiting London and we had someone to take care of the house and plants!

Wendy

19 general considerations

1

Nurseries may offer a gradual introductory process for settling in your child. With other types of care it will be up to you to think about the best approach for building the relationship between your child and their care.

2

Children often try to play adults off against each other to get the best deal. This might be worse when another adult is brought into the house, especially when they have supervisory responsibilities. There is a balance to be considered here – support the carer and show there is a consistency of approach and show your children that you listen to them and take their concerns seriously.

3

Some children may be inappropriately negative or critical towards their carer. One way to tackle this is to ask, "What have you done today to help their day?" This may be particularly helpful with au pairs who have to cope not only with children but a new country and language.

4

If the childcare is in your own home it can be tempting for some children to think of their carer as a kind of servant and make demands that fall well outside the call of duty. This is not good for anyone. If children have household chores they should continue to do them – it is their contribution to the home.

5

If your child care provider will be driving your children it is reasonable to ask if you can accompany them on a journey before they drive alone with their charges, to check that you are comfortable with their driving standards. If they are new to this country you may wish to ask them to drive without passengers for a period of time until they get used to the car and the roads.

6

If your childcare provider lives in and they have a TV or audio system in their room which may disturb others, you could ask them to turn it off at a specific time or request that they use headphones, which you should provide.

7

Knowing what you want and being able to explain this is a key foundation to the relationship. Express your expectations and ensure they are met. Talking these through is likely to be ongoing.

8

Younger children may become upset when you leave them – this is quite normal. A routine is helpful here. When you say you are going, go - and don't be tempted to come back a few minutes later. Be clear about your intentions and stick to them. Explain to the carer what your child prefers in terms of cuddles and favourite toys that will help to comfort. In a nursery this may be recorded so all carers are aware. Would a call be helpful to you to assure you all is well a short time after you have left? Popping in at the lunch break isn't a good idea as this may unsettle your child.

9

If you see behaviour from any of the children, including your own, that you might find worrying such as biting, hair pulling or scratching, consider the many different needs behind the behaviour. The child could be hungry, tired, or maybe jealous of a new baby. If it's your child, meet these needs and the behaviour should improve.

10

As a single parent, it is advisable to keep the carer informed of any change of circumstances. If the father is on the birth certificate then, unless of course there is a contrary court order, he is entitled to collect his child from a nursery or child minder. This sometimes puts nurseries and schools in a difficult position, so help by giving as much information as you feel comfortable divulging.

11

It may be that you and your child's father or mother has different views about the daily routine and care, when delegated to someone else, such as sleeping patterns and discipline. It will be helpful for both the carer and your child if these are resolved beforehand so there are no mixed messages.

12

Professional carers will expect children to go outside to play even in poor weather, so don't ask for them to stay in.

13

Don't be surprised if your carer encourages your children to do more for themselves than you have, such as pouring themselves a cold drink or dressing themselves. This may be a good thing.

14

Try to acclimatise your child to being able to sleep with background noise. This means you and the person looking after your child don't need to turn off the radio, television or the vacuum cleaner or stop others speaking or children playing.

15

Most children establish a sleeping pattern more easily if there is a routine and if this is what you are trying to do make sure whoever is looking after your child is aware of it.

16

Don't be surprised if you experience some pangs of jealousy if your child is affectionate towards the carer. This usually means that they have a good relationship so be reassured. Have confidence that your relationship with your child will always be the strongest.

17

If your child is invited to a party or other social occasion and you are not able to take them, ask the host if the carer can take them instead, in case they are expected to stay.

18

The reasons for your childcare of choice for your first child may not be as valid when it comes to your second or subsequent children. For example, if you have one child starting school you may now need someone who can drive. Someone who is good with toddlers may not necessarily be the best choice for a newborn or vice versa.

19

Show your appreciation occasionally to those looking after your child with some time off, a small gift or a bunch of flowers.

How's it going? 10 ways to find out

Once you have childcare in place this becomes a big question. Here are some suggested ways to find out.

1

Happiness of child

Is your child happy to see the carer? A reluctance to say goodbye to you is different from being unhappy with the carer. Has anything changed that you can't explain, such as eating and sleeping patterns? Do they seem withdrawn? Can the issues be resolved through discussion? Has enough adjustment time been given? Do you need to consider a change in care?

2

Cleanliness of child and environment

Is there basic hygiene and safety? Is it so sterile there is no evidence of play? Is it so chaotic it looks out of control?

3

Evidence of activity

If the child can talk, are they excited by what they have done? Can you see examples of a variety of play having taken place?

4

Willingness to talk

Is the carer positive about their work? Are they happy to talk about the day and any difficulties or concerns? Do you both make time to do this?

5

Keeping agreements

Is there evidence that what you have agreed will happen, is happening? Do they give you the feedback you have requested, keep you updated, and take your child to places as agreed?

6

Feedback from family/friends/neighbours who know your carer

Do you get a positive reaction when your carer is mentioned? If not, do you want to ask for their honest opinion, if you know they share similar views with you on childcare?

7

Popping in

Can you pop in unexpectedly sometime or ask a trusted person to do so? What observations are made?

8

Older siblings

Are you listening to them to understand their issues and perspectives? What views do they have on the carer? Do their concerns worry you or are they just playing adults off against each other?

9

Reports from nursery.

Are there written reports about your child's development? Do you have the opportunity to discuss them? Is your contribution welcomed?

10

Observing relationships.

Do you get a good feeling when you see your carer with your child? How does your child respond to them?

Personal Story

As someone who has recruited professionally for many years, I took the task of finding my first nanny very seriously. I was quite clear that I wanted a daily nanny as I felt our house wouldn't accommodate a live-in. I employed an ex-nurse, had a full week's induction plan worked out, introduced her to my neighbours, the doctor, set out training on the use of all the equipment in the house - you name it I had planned for it! My last week of maternity leave was spent with her to introduce her to my first-born and so I returned to work feeling very pleased that I had organised it all. Four days after I returned to work — she resigned, as she couldn't cope with being on her own with a baby. I was devastated and had one day to organise a replacement. I was only the second working mother in Head

Office in my role so I was determined that my work would not be affected. An agency offered me an experienced nanny who had taken two years off to travel. She didn't want to return to being a nanny but was prepared to cover for me for a couple of weeks whilst she thought about her future. However, it would only work if she could live in during the week. In the end, Amanda stayed for two years! Living in Monday to Friday worked perfectly and we continued with this type of arrangement for years. I helped Amanda identify her future career and supported her as she trained to become a midwife and we all went to her wedding a few years later. The lesson for me was that, whilst planning is important, being flexible is necessary and for all my criteria based interviewing techniques, I needed to trust my instincts more and ask myself "do I feel happy with this person looking after my child?" I had lost sight of this with the first appointment.

Wendy

Employers' and Colleagues' Perspectives

Be sensitive to the impact the demands of parenting may have on your work, colleagues and employer. Early warning, contingency plans and good communication are all vital. Here are 4 ways to be helpful to those you work with.

1

Arrange your child's medical appointments out of work hours or organise someone else to take them if it isn't urgent.

2

Have a back up in case your child care provider won't look after a sick child, is sick themselves or you can't get your child to them.

3

If you travel or work long hours with your job, then you may also need additional childcare. This extra support could be provided by friends so be prepared to ask them for help and reciprocate in what ever way you can.

4

Even with meticulous planning there will be times when the unexpected happens. Keep communication open with your employer and offer to compensate them in some way, such as offering some replacement hours or working from home

A Final Consideration

We believe children are very resilient and within reason can gain from a range of experiences. As long as we are the constant figures in our children's lives, the impact childcare can have is often less of a concern to them than it is to us. Those feelings of guilt and anxiety are very often ill founded. In spite of the turmoil you might be experiencing, if your child is happy and content, that is all that matters.

ADDITIONAL MATERIAL

- Ideas for inclusion in an advert for child care

- Suggested questions when interviewing a nanny/carer

- Letter of introduction: suggested content

- Suggested content for contract for an au pair

- Reference: sample content

Ideas for inclusion in an advert for child care

If looking for a nanny, then you may want to specify qualifications. They wouldn't normally do any housework unless it is associated with the children. Currently an au pair can only work five hours a day and will need to attend college to improve their English. Take a look at websites such as gumtree.com for sample adverts.

Select from the following.

- Start date

- Temporary or permanent, full or part-time

- Type of arrangement: live in/daily nanny/nanny share/child minder/ babysitter

- Hours of work

- Any extra duties required such as babysitting or cleaning

- Number, ages and gender of children

- Overview of expected duties

- Other expectations such as standard of English, valid passport, visa

- Holidays

- Salary

- Details of accommodation and meals provided

- Mention of pets

- Non-smoker required perhaps?

- Area and local transport links

- Whether a driver is preferred or essential

- Qualifications and/or experience required Whether the post is suitable for someone who is newly qualified

- How to reply – what information you require such as CV and references that you can follow up

- Contact details and date of closure for applications

Interviewing a nanny/carer

Suggested Questions
General
Get them talking. (To relax them and to get a picture of how they have behaved in past situations which is an indicator of how they might perform in post)
What do you enjoy most and least about looking after children? Or why do you want to look after children (if they are newly qualified)?
Tell me about the people you grew up with.
Talk me through your child caring experience. (For newly qualified this may be younger siblings, babysitting, work experience)
What is the biggest problem you have faced (in or out of work)?
Basic information, training and experience
(For a newly qualified nanny only) How much of your course was childcare focused (rather than on the parents)?
What experience have you had of being a nanny and being in a nursery (this could have been a placement if they are newly qualified)?

Are you first aid trained?
How would you deal with a choking child?

Do you smoke?

What type of food do you cook for children?

Please give details of your driving experience.
What absence have you had and for what reason?

What holiday commitments do you have?

Why are you leaving your current job?

When are you available to start?

Approach

Can you give me some examples of when you have
had to discipline a child?
How do you organise your time?

What methods do you use to ensure the children are
organised for school and other activities?

What gets you stressed? How do you react to this?
How do you communicate with your employers (by
what method and how often)?
What kind of household do you enjoy working in the
most? Why?

What issues might you face with X year old
boy/girl/s?

What activities do you enjoy with children?
What would you like to know about our children/child?
Personal qualities
How would your last employers describe you?
How would the children describe you?   What gets you cross?
What makes you laugh?   What do employers do that annoys you?

What to look for

Looking for specific examples of how they have handled different situations will give you valuable information. Asking "how have you .....?" gives more specific evidence rather than "what would you do if....?" This will help give you comfort that they have a similar approach to you. Clarify your own thoughts first about what is important to you regarding issues such as discipline, food, sleeping, potty training and sharing toys. If the candidate does have different views, discuss your own and see if they are prepared to adopt your approach. Each family will have different ideas and the nanny may have had to adjust and be flexible accordingly.

N.B. Nannies will also have a gut feeling about the family they might work with. If they are young and living away from home and not driving, adjusting to a new family can be quite hard.

Do always remember that the process is covered by the laws against unlawful discrimination on grounds of race, nationality and gender. Don't be afraid of these. Obviously you must not discriminate directly out of sheer prejudice. Just check that you can justify what you are asking for in a way that most people would consider even handed and fair.

Closing the interview

What questions would you like to ask?

From what you have heard, what interests you about this role?

Is there anything about yourself that you would like to add?

Explain what the process will be now – when you will tell them the result. Finish by thanking them for coming and explain what the process will be and how they will hear the outcome. You might consider offering to pay their travel expenses.

Letter of introduction for an au pair: suggested content

1. Welcome

2. Information about your children such as names, ages and interests in and out of school and pets

3. Information about yourselves, where you work, hours of work and interests

4. Where you live, facilities and amenities in the area

5. Information about colleges/tutors where they can study English

6. Basic outline of duties and expectations

7. Arrangements for weekends and holidays – will you want them involved with your family?

8. Opportunities for extra earning such as cleaning for other people

9. Au pair networks

10. Questions for them

Contract for au pair: suggested content

1. Welcome

2. Main responsibilities

3. Notice period

4. Holidays

5. Hours of work

6. Pocket money

7. Visitors

8. Smoking

9. Car travel

10. Registration

11. Medical treatment

12. Use of telephone and PC

13. Problems

14. Care responsibility

15. Signatures and date

A sample completed contract for an au pair can be found in Appendix B.

Reference: sample content

1. Your address and current date

2. Length of time they have worked for you

3. Outline of their responsibilities

4. Key skills and attributes

5. If applicable, relate their qualities and experience to the post they are applying for

Chapter Three

Making the Most of Your Time Away from Work

"Parenthood is a lot easier to get into than out of".

Bruce Lansky

Commonly known as 'maternity leave', this period of time away from work, before and after the birth, is really a period during which you retain a legal right to return to work. It is a precious time for looking after yourself and your baby.

Priorities that seemed clear prior to the birth can often change dramatically and this time is so useful in helping you to adjust. No matter how ready you feel you are, nothing can really prepare you for the birth of your first child. Parenting can feel very confusing and even overwhelming. We hope this chapter helps you to manage the physical and emotional changes, as well as providing some practical tips.

You may have heard that pregnancy can cause a woman's brain to be less efficient, with tales of forgetfulness and making silly mistakes. This may happen to you. However, it is likely to be temporary. There is a study at the University of Richmond, Virginia that shows that motherhood may actually boost female brainpower.

"Having a child rewires a woman's brain, improving her mental agility and health: "Pregnant women do undergo a phase of so-called baby brain, when they experience an apparent loss of function," said Craig Kinsley, Professor of Neuroscience at the University of Richmond, Virginia. "However, this is because their brains are being remodelled for motherhood to cope with the many new demands they will experience. "The changes that kick in then could last for the rest of their lives, bolstering cognitive abilities and protecting them against degenerative diseases."[1]

---

[1] *Jonathan Leake, Motherhood boosts female brain power, Timesonline Life & Style, reproduced from the Sunday Times, October 12, 2008.*

Wellbeing

5 ideas for before the birth

1

Listen to your body. Look after number one while you're pregnant. Your body will tell you when to rest so don't feel you are in some sort of competition to "soldier on" regardless. Admitting that you are tired is not a sign of weakness.

2

If you are used to being organised, you may have made many plans for your maternity leave. If your physical needs appear to be in conflict with these well-thought-out plans let your body be the winner!

3

Having a massage is a great way to relax. Do check that your masseur is qualified and has experience working with pregnant women. Some oils should not be used at this time so always check with a qualified therapist.

4

If you're used to having goals and objectives at work, consider growing your baby as your new purpose.

5

If you can, have a beauty treatment before the baby is born but check with your midwife whether your hospital expects you to have nail varnish removed before you go for the full manicure and pedicure!

And 10 for after the birth

1

Breastfeeding can be joyous, but it can also be tricky. Take advice from the professionals but be prepared for a variety of views and experiences. Don't put pressure on yourself – just do what you can and what feels right for you.

2

If breastfeeding is going well and you want to carry on once you've returned to work, then you can always express milk.

3

If your baby is happy to take from a bottle (formula and/or breast milk) you will have so much more flexibility. Maternity leave gives you a great opportunity to try this out.

4

If you have stitches after the birth try using the bath to wee in as it can reduce any discomfort enormously. Of course we suggest you do this at the end of your ablutions and not at the start! Alternatively try using a showerhead. A bidet is even more convenient.

5

Use a cool hair drier on stitches rather than a towel for greater comfort.

6

Keep your essential items nearby such as water, phone, changing bag, especially when you're feeding the baby to reduce the amount of getting up and walking around. This is particularly important if you are going to be on your own for long stretches of time. Get help from others to gather together the things you might need before they leave you on your own.

7

Sleep whenever you can! A good time is when your baby is asleep, resisting the temptation to get on with household tasks.

8

If you would like a beauty treatment or have your hair cut find out whether it can be done at home.

9

Eat well. Proper nutrition is really important for your recovery and, if you are breastfeeding, will also help your baby. If others ask how they can help, consider asking them to bring you a meal.

10

The shorter the maternity leave you have, the harder it may be to recover fully physically. We think it can take up to a year for your body to repair so avoid putting yourself under pressure to do things before you are ready.

Personal Story

Within two weeks of giving birth to my first son I found a temporary job doing a little office work at the National Foundation for Education Research. With education in the title it felt comfortable to be doing something other than looking after baby even if it wasn't teaching and I was able to take my son with me. I struggled to lug the wicker basket complete with baby up the several flights of stairs and did the paperwork for a few hours each week, while keeping an eye on my son. It was quite exhausting but somehow satisfied the urge to feel I was still a 'working' person. The task had little meaning and it didn't take long before I realised I really didn't need to prove anything, that looking after my child was important enough and that I would adjust to these changes of perceived status.

Penny

10 tips for emotional wellbeing

"You should not confuse your career with your life."
Dave Barry

1

Before your baby is born you may experience a strong desire to "nest" in the house. This can be as simple as wanting to rearrange some furniture to having a complete overhaul. If you must do something then prepare where the baby will sleep, but don't push things too far. Too much disruption can be exhausting and could put a strain on you or other family members.

2

Get a sense of perspective by having a list of priorities of what <u>must</u> be done in and around the house and adding what you would <u>like</u> to have done.

Spinning Yarns

Q: *Our baby was born last week.*

When will my wife begin to feel and act normal again?

A: *When the kids leave home.*

http://lifepassages.net/jokes.html

3

If you take time off work before the birth, you may feel a bit strange. You're not on holiday, the baby

105

hasn't arrived and you feel quite capable of doing some work. This is a transition phase – however long – towards being a mother. Think carefully before going about business as usual.

4

Having a baby can be very overwhelming and you may well experience contrasting emotions ranging from great love to enormous fear, from paralysing anxiety to blissful contentment. You may feel a loss of status or that you are coming adrift from your identity as a working person. Reframe this thinking. Try thinking about yourself as a working person who is also now a parent. This is a reason to really feel good about yourself, not upset.

5

As a working woman, used to being in control - this could be the first time you have ever asked anyone other than your parents for help and it can be a great learning experience. No one will think less of you. If they do, ignore them! Don't expect to work everything out for yourself. Most people are actually very willing to help and love to be asked. It's fine to learn from others to do the most important job on earth.

6

Maternity leave gives you the opportunity to be at home and establish new connections and friends. This isn't always possible when you're working so seize the chance. You may get great support from this new network. Your health visitor, other expectant mothers, your neighbours can all be a great source of useful contacts.

7

Be aware of the expectations you have of your partner. They may not be able to provide all the emotional support you need, as they have their own adjustments to make. Ask for what you need and remember friends and family can help too.

8

We think most mothers feel vulnerable about the decisions they are making about returning to work, which means that comments from others about this can be heard as criticism, when it may not be. It is perfectly normal to feel unsure about these decisions we are making. Be authentic about your feelings. See 'Things People Say' box, at the end of this chapter.

Personal Story

I took voluntary redundancy after my second son was born and found myself with a toddler and baby in a village where I had not forged links or made friends, as I used to go to work in the dark and come home in the dark! The mums I had made friends with whilst pregnant, didn't go out to work and had forged new relationships. My husband was working abroad much of the week and I had turned from an independent working mum to a far more fragile person who was struggling to cope. I visited my very wonderful health visitor, Celia, to say that I thought I was depressed. She wisely counselled me to think through my feelings and helped to recognise that actually I was in the process of grieving — for my professional self. I was very glad that I sought professional help and was fortunate that I wasn't suffering from depression, as can often happen post-natally. For me, by accepting this emotional state, I could work through my feelings and recognise that it was a transition that I needed to go through- and I did.

Wendy

9

Make the effort to get to know any other pregnant women you meet. If you restrict yourself to only connecting with working parents you may be missing out on some great friendships with those who have chosen not to return to work.

10

Watch out for some irrational thinking! Penny's first son was born in mid October and she truly believed that she would never again attend any Bonfire Night celebrations. The whole world seemed to have changed and she couldn't imagine being able to take part in this annual celebration. Needless to say she's been enjoying 5th November celebrations every year since. She also remembers staring at lamp-posts on her way home from hospital with her first child and being amazed they hadn't changed. Clearly everything else had in her life at that time.

8 Relationship Tips

1

Be prepared for some changes in your relationships. Penny is in a very egalitarian marriage, yet having a child resulted in a large shift to a more traditional sharing of roles – most of it willingly! If this happens to you, be aware that it might continue once you're back at work and you could end up taking on so many more tasks. We both surprised ourselves by choosing, unprompted, to take on the domestic tasks associated with looking after our children and our homes. Be honest with yourself, ask for support when you need it, and do avoid slipping into feelings of martyrdom.

2

We found that older children seemed to need us even more as they reached adolescence and beyond, than when they were very small. At this stage you might wish to be even more involved in their lives given the many pressures experienced by young people. This might affect your decision about returning to work when your baby is tiny as their needs, which are mainly physical, can be more easily met by another caring person. Perhaps you can gradually work less as they get older.

3

After your first child, you might wonder if you would be able to love another child as much as the first. Don't worry; there is no limitation on love!

4

The instinctive protection you feel for a new baby can sometimes cause negative feelings towards your older children, especially if they appear threatening to the new arrival. Accept these feelings and try to understand how the older child is feeling. Nurture the relationship and spend time alone with them whenever you can.

5

Other parents are vital to talk to but don't make parenting your only topic of conversation. Seek out those with wider interests too and give yourself a balance.

6

Maternity leave is an ideal time to establish healthy relationships with the person who will be looking after your child, family members and even friends. Be careful you don't manage the relationship with your carer as if they were a work colleague. Use the skills you have such as delegation, communication and mentoring but remember this will be a very different relationship you are building.

7

Family and friends may think they can say what they like about your choice of childcare or they may feel they shouldn't say anything. Make it clear whether you want any feedback. You will want to know if the issue is to do with the child's wellbeing but think about any other areas you might like their opinions on.

8

Be aware of the way in which close family members relate to the person who will be looking after your child. They could be over-friendly, disapproving, critical or even interfering. Be clear about the way you hope they will interact and then ask for their support.

6 practical tips for before the birth

1

It may sound obvious, but if you have the choice, avoid having builders in or moving house. You have quite enough to cope with.

2

Set up an account with an online supermarket and register with other retailers if you haven't done so already.

3

Babies don't always arrive when planned which can mean maternity leave before the birth is shorter than you had hoped for, so buy the essentials in plenty of time.

4

Have you thought about these questions? Who will take care of the older siblings? How will you get to hospital? What if you need to go in the middle of the night? What if you have to have the baby at home?

Personal Story

Wise words from my mum — despite her very strong desire to be on the doorstep when I arrived home from hospital and to move in, she very wisely suggested that Neil should be with me for his paternity leave as soon as we got home, rather than a few weeks later when a routine was established. This was so we could learn the first steps of being parents together, with all the mistakes and worries that come with it. For example, the first time our baby cried when we got home, Neil asking: "why is he crying" and me saying: "I don't know, I met him the same time you did"! Three weeks later, once Neil had gone back to work, my mum did come to stay and that was a great help.

Wendy

5

Have lots of cheap baby clothes — consider second hand — and save the beautiful things for rare occasions so that you're not stressed about ruining expensive outfits.

6

Despite the romantic image, don't be tempted to take pristine white, delicate nightclothes to hospital — easy wash is what is needed here! If you want to have something that makes you feel feminine then how about a lovely shawl or a top that you can put on?

And 4 for after the birth

1

Don't try to be a 'Supermum'! In spite of your brilliant multi-tasking abilities and fabulous organisational skills this is a time when asking for help is a sign of strength, not weakness. - we know we've said this before but it's really important. If you have ever met a new mum who was perfectly turned out with an immaculate house and contented baby, we reckon that once you left she probably collapsed in tears with exhaustion!

2

Create a list of jobs that need doing, pin it up and when visitors come and ask what they can do, get them to choose something from the list. Decide what job you least want to do such as ironing or hanging out the washing and suggest someone else does this for you. Well, why not??

3

Perhaps someone could take your baby out for a walk so if they cry, you won't hear them and you can get a proper rest. Be sure to turn off phones too!

4

Pay a trusted teenager to pop in for an hour a day to sit with an older child or watch the baby while you have a bath, tidy up or just take some time out. This is especially helpful if you have more than one child.

The 'Middle Wife' by an Anonymous 2nd grade teacher.

I've been teaching now for about fifteen years. I have two kids myself, but the best birth story I know is the one I saw in my own second grade classroom a few years back. When I was a kid, I loved show-and-tell. So I always have a few sessions with my students. It helps them get over shyness and usually, show-and-tell is pretty tame. Kids bring in pet turtles, model airplanes, pictures of fish they catch, stuff like that. And I never, ever place any boundaries or limitations on them. If they want to lug it in to school and talk about it, they're welcome.

Well, one day this little girl, Erica, a very bright, very outgoing kid, takes her turn and waddles up to the front of the class with a pillow stuffed under her sweater. She holds up a snapshot of an infant. 'This is Luke, my baby brother, and I'm going to tell you about his birthday.' 'First, Mom and Dad made him as a symbol of their love, and then Dad put a seed in my Mom's stomach, and Luke grew in there. He ate for nine months through an umbrella cord.'

She's standing there with her hands on the pillow, and I'm trying not to laugh and wishing I had my camcorder with me. The kids are watching her in amazement. 'Then, about two Saturdays ago, my Mom starts saying and going, 'Oh, Oh, Oh, Oh!' Erica puts a hand behind her back and groans. 'She walked around the house for, like an hour, 'Oh, oh, oh!' (Now this kid is doing a hysterical duck walk and groaning.)

'My Dad called the middle wife. She delivers babies, but she doesn't have a sign on the car like the Domino's man. They got my Mom to lie down in bed like this.' (Then Erica lies down with her back against the wall.) 'And then, pop! My Mom had this bag of water she kept in there in case he got thirsty, and it just blew up and spilled all over the bed, like psshhheew!' (This kid has her legs spread with her little hands miming water flowing away. It was too much!)

'Then the middle wife starts saying 'push, push' and 'breathe, breathe'. They started counting, but never even got past ten. Then, all of a sudden, out comes my brother. He was covered in yucky stuff that they all said it was from Mom's play-center, (placenta) so there must be a lot of toys inside there. When he got out, the middle wife spanked him for crawling up in there.'

Then Erica stood up, took a big theatrical bow and returned to her seat. I'm sure I applauded the loudest. Ever since then, when it's show-and-tell day, I bring my camcorder, just in case another 'Middle Wife' comes along.

www.funny.com

7 points from the child's perspective

1

Think about how your older children might feel when it comes to where the baby will sleep or sit. It's important they don't feel pushed out of their space and place in the family and home. Don't assume they will be happy with the choice you made to have another child.

2

Think about how you are going to introduce older children to the new baby. Perhaps you can leave your hospital bed and greet your older child, at the end of the corridor. If you are confined to bed maybe a family member, friend or one of the nursing staff could move the baby just until you have spent a little time with your older children. Show your older children just how pleased you are at seeing them rather than the visit being solely about them meeting the baby.

3

A small gift from the baby for the older child works well. Don't assume the older child will fall in love with the baby. It's perfectly normal if they don't.

4

From the older child's perspective having a new sibling is a bit like the following: "A husband brings home another wife and expects his first wife to love her, share her home, clothes and even bedroom with her, take care of her and find pleasure in watching the husband show her affection." Imagine how we might react to that!

5

If you are concerned about your older child's behaviour towards the new baby, try to understand the needs behind the behaviour. They might be feeling rejected and therefore angry. Do talk to someone about this. Health visitors can be a good source of support and information on these kinds of issues.

6

Spend time with older children when you can and get someone else to look after the baby.

7

Help older children to express their feelings about adjusting to the new dynamics of their family. At the age of five, Penny's older son expressed very clearly his confusion about thinking he was in a family of three and now it was four. Just articulating his thoughts helped him to adjust more easily.

World of Work

"Nothing is really work unless you would rather be doing something else".

J.M. Barrie

The decision to return to work

Personal Story

I couldn't decide what would work until I had tried going back full time — my thinking was it would be easier to scale down than up. I also felt that I would be unhappy if I stayed at home but also unhappy if I went back to work (missing either my child or my work) but that if I went back to work at least I would be paid whilst unhappy! I have also found that when the children were little I missed them, but as long as they had good care and got to see me and my husband regularly they were fine. It was when they got older that they specifically wanted my input (and I wanted to be more involved) and therefore I worked full time when they were babies and reduced my hours as they got older. Each of us will have differing views on this and the pull to stay with the baby can be strong, but know that if you have assessed all the options and make a choice — it doesn't have to be permanent. You may not even have a choice — in which case accepting and making the most of it may be a trite but sensible approach.

Wendy

Your decision to return to work will probably be based on one or more of the following:

- How you feel
- Health issues
- Financial consideration
- Child care options
- Flexibility and alternatives at work
- Partner support
- Career direction

Here are 8 pointers

1

How you feel is obviously very personal. We have heard many say it's a 50:50 decision. If you find yourself in this position try thinking that if you go back to work, at least you are being paid! Also, if you do return, you will be in a better position to make an informed decision about what suits you best.

2

Wendy read a great article about how going out to work has no negative impact on your child's intelligence but we've been unable to track it down.

3

One financial consideration is to check whether your child care costs will be covered sufficiently by your projected earnings.

4

If you have explored with your employer already your options for returning to work, you may feel ready to negotiate your return. The options available to you may help you decide.

5

It may be helpful to request reduced hours when you first return to work, especially if you are still breast feeding. It may then be possible for your hours to be increased at a later date.

6

We know of families where partners have been willing and able to adjust their working hours to provide some of the child care.

7

If you choose to take a career break now is it possible for you to return at a later date on the same salary level or position?

8

Another consideration may be school fees. If your decision to return to work is based on helping to pay for school fees, it may be that children, who know this, can feel under huge pressure to "deliver" to your expectations. Sending your child to a fee-paying school is your choice. It should not be their burden. We believe there is also no guarantee that private schools will deliver a better education. The only likely guarantee is a smaller class size.

3 tips from the employer's perspective

1

While you are on maternity leave, do let your employer know what, when and how often you would like to be updated with what is happening at work.

2

Keep them informed as soon as you can if your situation changes in any way.

3

If you wish to negotiate any changes to your employment on your return, it is helpful to both parties to meet face to face rather than telephone or e-mail.

3 tips on preparing to return to work

1

Consider the best way to keep in touch with work and why you want to. Emails can be helpful but it may be that you'll need to attend an occasional meeting. If you are yet to organise permanent child care this can be hard but sometimes talking face to face and setting foot in the work place can give you confidence about returning. Perhaps your partner/family member/neighbour can help out. If you do have child care in place this is the perfect opportunity for you all to have a trial run.

2

As you prepare your return you may wish to arrange to receive work calls at home at a pre-arranged time or for you to return calls at your convenience. This ensures that you are able to focus on the call rather than trying to juggle home and work.

3

If returning to your original work is proving pretty impossible, then be encouraged by the growing number of successful female entrepreneurs who have decided to set up their own businesses, to work around their families' needs. More of this in Chapter Five.

Personal Story

I planned to return to work full time six months after having my first baby but when the time came I really didn't feel ready so I asked for two more months. I was surprised by my feelings but felt unable to leave my baby or to travel and stay overnight once a month, which would have been expected of me. Even then I was still not ready to do full time so I asked if I could do three to four days per week. My boss said he needed to think about it as he could possibly restructure. He then rang me to say 'no'. It was so tough to hear this over the phone especially as I was asked for my notice in writing and I was very distressed.

I came up with an idea to put a new proposal to the company and asked for a face to face meeting. I suggested a new role for myself, offered to take a pay cut and requested three days only. It was agreed I should take on less work, earn less money pro rata but would have less responsibility. This new job has subsequently grown. At first I did two days a week in the office and one at home but the amount of time commuting reduced with my second pregnancy. Now my new role has been made a permanent role rather than temporary. I have even been offered the chance to do some of the work while on maternity leave and be paid for it! Looking back I realise how hard it is to negotiate for yourself and, as a result, I undervalued my contributions, ending up with less money as a result. I wish I could have been able to negotiate for myself. At the time I needed to know what my rights were and whose job it was to know them. There seemed to be little creativity *used to find ways through. The original position I held has still not been filled. I am concerned about the loss of some very good, experienced women in the workplace who, unlike me, were unable to negotiate fewer working hours. I believe it is wrong to feel grateful for flexibility! It also seems that without an HR department, companies flounder when handling maternity leave. The element of trust is essential between employee and employer in this new relationship and I know that I am trusted by my employer to make up any time I need to take, if my child is ill for example. On reflection, my tips for others are:*

✗ *Go back to work for a rest. (At least at work you have time to go to the loo or have a coffee!)*

✗ *Don't undervalue yourself*

✗ *Don't be worried about presenting options*

✗ *Don't feel guilty*

✗ *9.00am -5.30pm would not have worked for me — flexibility has made parenting and working enjoyable*

✗ *Use your 10 'KIT' (Keeping In Touch) days to keep up to date and be paid*

✗ *Utilise technology to enable you to work from home*

✗ *Working from home (with childcare) really helpful*

✗ *Opportunities to return to original post*

Anonymous

Things People Say – and some responses

(Beware of using a sarcastic tone, whatever you say!)

We have either been on the receiving end or have heard the following said to others about their decision to return to work. It's a great help to have some rehearsed responses for such a time when you may be feeling a little unsure of how it will all work out. In general it helps to be straight about how you feel, without having to justify your thoughts or be defensive. The following may be useful in a variety of situations. "I don't know how I will feel about going back to work unless I try it. No decision is forever." You will find the 'Things People say' in the first column. In the second column are some suggestions for your responses, which are assertive, non-aggressive and non-judgmental. In the third column are some suggestions of what you'd probably like to say but really shouldn't!!!!

Making The Most Of Your Time Away From Work

Things People Say	Helpful Responses	Think – Don't Say!
"You'll miss him when you go back to work."	"Yes, I will."	"Nah! At least at work I'll get a cup of coffee!"
"You won't be able to leave him with just anyone you know."	"Yes, I have given it a great deal of thought. Do you have any ideas that I haven't considered?"	"Funny, I hadn't thought of that."
"I suppose you know what you are doing."	"As it's our first time, we're not entirely sure that we have everything covered, but we have given it a lot of thought."	"Never have so far!"
"I don't know how you could go back to work and leave him."	"It is going to be tough."	"You have him for a while then you'll see!"
"I couldn't do that."	"We are all different."	"No, you probably couldn't."
"What's the point in having children if you are going to let someone else bring them up?"	"I'll always be their Mum."	"I've always been good at delegating."
"Have you seen the film, "The hand that rocks the cradle?"	"I have – dreadful film/loved it – so funny", "I haven't, but I hear it's a dreadful dramatisation."	"Yes, weren't you in it?"
"You hear such horror stories about child care these days."	"I don't listen to those tales. We are taking great care when choosing our child care."	"I know, children can be so cruel."
"I never thought you'd have children."	"I'm so glad I have."	"They let anyone these days."
"Why don't you wait until they go to school?"	"This is the decision we've made for now."	"Because the schools round here don't take them until they are 4 and

Things People Say	Helpful Responses	Think – Don't Say!
		I can't wait until then."
"I never left my children."	"We are all different."	"I know, and look how they turned out."
"I'm lucky I didn't have to go back to work."	"I'm looking forward to going back." Or, "I feel ok about returning."	"Yeah, your boss was lucky too."
"It would be better if you had family to look after them."	"Well, it would be different."	"Have you met my mother?"
"I take my hat off to you."	"Thank You!"	"So you should."
"I don't know how you'll manage."	"Nor do I yet, and we'll let you know."	"Badly, probably."

Chapter Four

Returning to Work – Personal Adjustment

"My Mother is a travel agent for guilt trips".

Ruby Wax

Even after just a holiday we can feel a little nervous returning to work, so having had the life changing experience of birth, the emotional highs and lows, the physical changes and then deciding to leave the baby behind – no wonder we feel "different" and perhaps a little anxious.

Be in tune with your inner self so that you can be clear about the decision you have made to go back to work. This will help you respond to the perceptions and opinions others may have of working mothers.

This chapter will help remind you who you are given the huge changes in your life and help you feel more confident that you are doing the best for yourself, your family and your work.

"Too often we decide to follow a path that is not really our own, one that others have set for us. We forget that whichever way we go, the price is the same: in both cases, we will pass through both difficult and happy moments. But when we are living our dream, the difficulties we encounter make sense."
Paulo Coelho

On preparing to return

"Courage is a quality you develop. Some people think that courage is something that you are born with. However, courage is something you develop by taking on increasingly larger challenges with the same or even greater enthusiasm. Courage is really about taking action on the unknown, and action is always the fuel for your courage."

Mark Fritz

Emotional

"Nobody can make you feel inferior without your permission"
Eleanor Roosevelt

Emotional confusion can come from a variety of sources and, when you have a baby there can be many conflicting thoughts around your career, relationships, desire to stay with the baby, fear of loss of status and other concerns such as financial ones. Unless we acknowledge the pull that we feel in returning to work as a mother, we may struggle with the emotional turmoil.

A lack of confidence when returning to work after having a baby appears to be common. Why is this? It may come from the significant shift in priorities. Where we had once been so clear and focused at work, there is now something of greater importance in our lives. The struggle to come to terms with that and then embrace both work and parenthood, may be the underlying reduction in our confidence. It might simply be about our nurturing instincts. Indeed, we have both admitted to each other that we still have occasional pangs as we reflect on the feelings generated by separation from our children as we returned to work. However, we have learned to accept these feelings and remain confident about the decisions we have made.

"You probably wouldn't worry about what people think of you if you could know how seldom they do."

Olin Miller

Here are 5 points to help you manage your feelings

1

Accept your decision or need to return to work. It will help reduce personal stress and anxiety. Ask yourself the questions "Why are you working?" The reasons might be financial, independence, intellectual stimulation, career development or social needs. Free yourself by identifying your particular motive and accept it.

2

If you find that at times you doubt your ability to return to work, think about your past achievements and all your strengths. You applied and were recruited to do a job so remind yourself of the abilities, skills and experiences that qualified you to do the job in the first place. Try working through the following process:

a) **Situation** – think of a specific example where you have tackled an issue or felt a sense of achievement, such as organising a meeting or dealing with a difficult colleague.

b) **What I did** – describe the actions you took to make it happen.

c) **Result** – describe what happened, think about the before and after.

d) **Skills** – what skills and qualities did you use? These may include planning and organising, assertiveness, persuading and influencing, negotiation, communication, I.T., technical knowledge, empathy, and listening.

3

Look for support in helping to build your confidence from those that know and care about you. Share how you are feeling.

4

Don't be surprised if you feel overwhelmed about leaving your child – or even if you don't! You can experience a whole range of emotions from guilt, fear, anxiety and even pleasure! You may feel dreadful leaving your baby – and you may not. Your feelings are valid and are just feelings. Whatever you feel is fine, and whatever you feel will probably change – sometimes hourly.

5

Prepare for the negative comments of others and have your response ready. See the last chapter. Face it, accept it, take action and allow time to pass.

With so much to think about and to organise, have a conversation with your partner about the changes that returning to work might bring for you both. Don't assume that there will be an understanding of the implications. Some of the issues may also be relevant to discuss with older children.

Ideas to discuss:

- What are your expectations of each other?

- Who will be the main point of contact with the person looking after your child?

- Who will get the child ready in the morning?

- Who will manage the handover morning and evening?

- Who will prepare food and clothes for the next day?

- Who will be the emergency contact with the carer?

- Who will take a day off if the child is unwell or has any appointments?

- If one of you is travelling away from home, to what extent can you be interrupted?

- How can you support each other? Practically and emotionally?

- Will there need to be changes to the running of the home?

- Can you make time to review how it is working for you on a regular basis?

Personal Story

When they were tiny I felt I missed them dreadfully but as long as they were cuddled, loved, fed, clean etc and saw Neil and me on a regular basis they were fine about us not being there all the time, so I preferred working full time as they were little and worked part time as they got older.

Wendy

7 practical ways to help with your return to work

1

What do you need to do to bring yourself up to date before you return? This shouldn't be a huge project in itself but can help build confidence if you are familiar with aspects such as business figures, changes to policy and new staff.

2

Arrange to have coffee or lunch with work colleagues, without the baby, before you return to work.

3

Arrange to go back to work on a Thursday so you only have to manage the return to work for two days before you catch your breath!

4

In the same vein, you could book a holiday to take shortly after you return as long as this doesn't cause too much inconvenience for your work colleagues.

5

Reduce stress in the mornings by getting up that bit earlier and having your clothes ready the night before.

6

It may help to reduce other activities and commitments for a while, to allow yourself to focus on work and being with baby at home but do explain to your partner that this is what you are trying to do.

7

In the morning put a light, easily washable dressing gown over work clothes, so if the baby deposits something unpleasant on you, you can simply take off the dressing gown. Keep it on until you have actually said your last goodbye – but do remember to take it off before you set off for work!

10 tips for looking after yourself

1

Don't be afraid to take care of yourself, as this is a way of modelling what you want for your child.

2

Will you express milk during the day? Where will you store it? How will you label it so your colleagues don't have it in their coffee? Where can you be undisturbed? Wendy even expressed milk on an aeroplane!

3

Take a break! Look after yourself! Book a beauty treatment soon after you have gone back to work.

4

Make the most of the gap between home and work.
Perhaps park near the house and collect your thoughts
before you go in, or use the train ride. Take this time
to reflect on your day and think about how your
children have spent theirs.

5

Have a snack as soon as you get home to help your
mood and lift energy levels.

6

The length of maternity leave can influence how you
feel when you go back. Don't be hard on yourself.

7

Tiredness and feeling low can be an issue for working
mums as you adjust physically and emotionally. It is
not a weakness. Often we ignore how we feel in an
attempt to prove that we are coping. Recognise this,
accept how you feel and get what sleep you can!
However if you tend to sleep on the train do set your
phone alarm!

8

If you think you may have post-natal depression seek
medical help as soon as possible.

9

Eat! Nutrition has been linked to our emotional state, so remember to eat well. Plan ahead by making use of your freezer and preparing nutritious packed lunches.

10

Build in time to keep fit to help you feel good. You could take a walk in your lunch break and those pelvic floor exercises can be done pretty much anywhere!

Personal Story

When I first had my daughter (now in her twenties), I was working in publishing — I had unrealistic expectations of getting back to work — particularly as I had not quite taken on board the physical effects of breastfeeding. When Anna was a few weeks old, I insisted that I could manage a visit to a well-known author, which involved accompanying a camera crew to her house. The idea back in the dark days of the early 80s was to carry on as if the baby has not affected your life in any way — I think we called it professionalism rather than what it really was — stupidity! - I met up with the four BBC guys (and back then of course they were all guys) in a pub on the outskirts of Newcastle. By the time I joined them my boobs were at bursting point so after ordering a drink I planned to disappear and do some expressing - I gripped my briefcase to make my escape to the ladies — too late I realised that it was not properly closed and in my haste to make a quick exit, I knocked it onto the wonderful old flagstone floor where it flew open. Three odd shaped pieces of my trusty breast pump skittered across the floor right to the feet of the best looking crewmember. Before I could do anything, he picked them up, held them up so his mates could get a good view and exclaimed so the whole pub could hear: 'What on earth are these?' I muttered something, grabbed them from him and ran......the rest of the day passed without incident and for me, in a haze of deep embarrassment. How life has changed. If that had happened today, I'm sure my daughter would say. 'Haven't you ever seen a breast pump before?' and the red face would be his not hers.

Wendy Boatman

8 thoughts to help you during your working day

"My work probably wouldn't be as good if I didn't have kids. It made me go down a road of serious self-examination. I think it's informed — and hopefully enhanced — my creativity. Motherhood was the beginning of my own spiritual journey, asking the question, "Why am I here?" I had to stop and think, "What am I going to teach my daughter? What do I believe in?" I decided to think beyond my career, beyond what I did for myself as an artist. Motherhood was my triggering point for trying to understand the true meaning of life."

Madonna

You may feel refreshed and reinvigorated about your work after a period of maternity leave. This means you could be more enthusiastic and more productive as a result. You may also have a different approach to work, maybe a new perspective that helps you with prioritising and decision-making, and some clear thinking about what is really important to you. At the very least, having a baby can certainly enhance your organisational skills.

> **"Your Attitude is Simply a Choice"**
>
> *Too many people say, "I will be happy when...", and are always expecting others to make them happy. Your happiness and your attitude are really not dependent on others, but simply a choice to make. You shape your world around you based on your attitude, and the attitude you enter the world in each day is your choice.*
>
> *Mark Fritz*

1

If someone does show an interest in your new status as a mother, don't take this as the chance to pin them against the wall while you give them all the details about your episiotomy scar and how your child can now manage an extra ounce of expressed milk!

2

Be bold about your diary and encourage others to respect your commitments. Ask for plenty of warning of any changes to dates and times for meetings and appointments.

3

Some colleagues seemed to have no difficulty in taking two hours for lunch and then later commenting "Oh, going home now are you?" to someone who has taken a very short lunch and leaves on time. Ignore it, use humour, or at the very least know that you are quite comfortable with your contribution.

4

If working late is difficult for you, perhaps you could work as late as you need to one night a week and go home on time the rest of the week.

5

Find a supportive colleague who can help you with the "we need to finish this meeting" notion.

6

It is common to feel that you might not be doing either parenting or working as well as you could if you only had one of these roles to concentrate on. Accept this and focus on which ever one you are engaged in at the time.

7

Changes at work will have taken place during your absence so give yourself time to adjust.

8

You may also have changed in your approach to work. For example you may wish to defer a promotion, which you might have jumped at before having a family. Consider whether your reasons are valid or simply a temporary lack of confidence. Don't let the latter stop you! Equally you may consider a reduction in your current responsibilities would suit you for a time.

Personal Story

If I were 30 minutes late getting home from work I would often have missed AJ's bath time and sometimes bedtime, so being three hours late one night a week made no difference. It allowed me to get home at the crucial "deadline" the other nights. Perhaps plan more meetings for your "late day" so you don't worry if they over run.

Wendy

"Those who believe they can do something are probably right — and so are those who believe they can't."

Unknown

Personal Story

What pressure are you putting yourself under trying to do it all? If you can find a good short cut — find it! Be careful of the dark thought that if you weren't working you would be doing all those extra things just perfectly - such as making the cake by hand. For example when my eldest had his first birthday I stayed up half the night making a Swiss roll for his train cake simply because the thought occurred that if I'd been at home I might have done this. A bought Swiss roll would have been fine and I could still have chosen to decorate it. Sometimes we impose standards on ourselves that are unreasonable.

Penny

If your work involves travelling consider the following 7 ideas

1

How can you minimise the jobs to be done at home? Wendy managed most things when her husband was away travelling three nights a week even though she worked and had two small children. However, having put the children to bed, tidied up, got ready for the next day and a myriad of other chores, watering the hanging baskets last thing at night (often in the dark) could reduce her to tears. Hanging baskets were one thing too many and should have been dispensed with for a couple of years. What is your "one thing too many"?

2

Identify the best time in the day or evening for both you and other family members to talk on the phone while you're away so that you can all be relaxed and enjoy the chat.

3

Make good use of technology to keep in contact such as text messages, e-mail and Skype.

4

Contingency plans for childcare are even more important if you are working away so have lots of back-up plans for unforeseen events such as sickness.

5

Leave notes under children's pillows wishing them goodnight and telling them how much you love them.

6

Don't forget to enjoy the time you have while you're away such as having a leisurely, luxurious bath, getting up later, reading or simply watching TV.

7

Reduce stress and effort when packing with a good list and by sticking to one main colour for your basic outfits.

"And my adage is - you can have two working parents but only one can travel extensively for the family and marriage to work!"

Bev Davis

3 tales of when worlds collide!

1

While away on a business trip a female friend with young children at home was sitting at an elegant dinner one evening. Chatting amiably to those around her, she absent-mindedly leaned across to her neighbour's plate and cut the meat up for the bemused colleague into bite-sized pieces!

2

Penny was working away from home and a little anxious about how the family were managing, although she had organised as much as she could beforehand. During the lunch break on the first day of a training course she was delivering she received a call from her teenage son. Fearing the worst and mentally working out how soon she could be back home if needed, she listened to her son as he asked, "Do you have any ideas what I can have for lunch?"

3

Wendy was running an assessment centre, which was a very pressurised four days away with very little spare time. Snatching a moment to call home she was told by her husband that he wanted to sack the nanny. Bracing herself to hear of some great misdemeanour, Wendy found out it was because the nanny hadn't tidied up the house properly!

Employer's perspective

3 things to consider that an employer will appreciate

1

Take the time to familiarise yourself with any changes that have taken place. Take responsibility by using contacts to update yourself.

2

Show that your period of maternity leave hasn't affected your enthusiasm and capabilities. You can do this by making sure you are punctual, interested and willing to take on new projects.

3

If a personal appointment during the day is unavoidable, give lots of notice and think through how your work can be covered. If reasonable notice can't be given, acknowledge others who have covered for you and look to reciprocate where possible.

*"Don't be a Stepford mother. Kids are like Ikea furniture —
you have no idea how much assembly is required until it's too
late. Perfect mothers exist only in American sitcoms."*

Kathy Lette

9 points from the children's perspective

1

When you do say goodbye to the baby – even when
they are very young, be clear and congruent, as babies
soon pick up on any hesitancy about you wanting to
leave.

2

Don't hurry when leaving and arriving home. Rushing
can make everyone feel more agitated, so allowing
extra time will be worth it.

3

It may be helpful for you to have a conversation with
your children about your needs as you are about to
return to work and the impact it's likely to have on
them.

4

Don't be surprised if each child responds differently to
the changed demands on your time. You may need to
make adjustments regarding the best way to spend
time with each one. For example, if something was

bothering Wendy's children, one was quite happy to wait to talk to her, whereas another needed her immediate attention.

5

Help your child understand how to reach you at work. What are the rules for calling?

6

You child care provider's working hours are a very important issue. If you do not get back to pick up your child at the agreed time, it can cause great upset – unless it is a rare occurrence.

7

Sharing stories about your day helps children feel involved and encourages them to share their day with you.

8

As the children grow older and your working patterns change, you may need to talk through further adjustments.

9

As a working parent, you will have provided a very positive role model. You will have given them an insight into the world of work and your experiences. There may be financial advantages as well as helpful contacts, networks and opportunities for them in the future. Your children may even feel proud of you for working and tell you so!

11 extra childcare tips

Chapter 2 focuses on child care but here are additional tips for the time you are returning to work.

1

Have a clear discussion about one another's expectations of the way things will work. View this as a job share – you are sharing the care of your child so build in communication time.

2

Have a book to exchange the day's happenings and comments such as what they have eaten that day, any new skills and what they enjoyed.

3

Make sure there is access to all your child's essentials such as clothes, play things, medication and food.

4

Essential information needs to be given and updated such as details of medical history, doctor's contacts, important family members and friends.

5

Explain to your child care provider how to reach you at work and any guidelines.

6

Establish agreements on issues that are important to you such as their diet and rules around activities such as eating and watching television.

7

Make your preferences on discipline clear. What do you feel about potty training? Would you insist on a complete "no smacking" rule? Your views need to be taken seriously, whereas other issues might be more open for discussion.

8

Take advice from child care professionals if you wish. However, your values regarding the upbringing of your child are paramount.

9

If the baby gets distressed when you are leaving for work, have faith they will be fine and just go! In most cases they will be fine and if for any reason they are not, ensure someone knows to call you.

10

Respect your carer's time. You may want to have a chat when you get home but this may still feel like "work" for them. If you need to talk, check when it is convenient with them, unless it is really urgent.

11

Consider how much contact you want with your carer during your time at work as you adjust to your return. You may need more reassurance at certain times such as during those first few days back at work or if your child has been unwell.

Personal Story

One of the most successful things we implemented was to have a diary where we asked nanny to include a summary of our child's day including sleeps, activities, outings and food. I still have it now and have read it several times with fond memories. Doesn't have to be a lot of information but it helped us!

Bev Davis

Personal Story

I remember one of the first Executive meetings I attended when I had returned to work after my first baby. It was an all male meeting (apart from me) and it was over running to the point where I would miss seeing my son before the nanny put him to bed and I really struggled to say I needed to leave. Then one of my colleagues announced, "Ok got to go – I'm off to the theatre tonight and can we finish?" Everyone agreed and the meeting finished. I realised I had assumed that if I made the request for the meeting to finish that people would think I wasn't as committed as them. Once I acknowledged to myself I could be a great worker and still be a mother, I gained more confidence in declaring what I needed.

Wendy

Returning to work after a longer break

If you are wishing to return to work after a longer break from employment consider the following questions:

- Where would you like to see yourself in 10 years' time? Will the goals you have set allow you to get there?

- What is your real priority in returning to work? Will your chosen route deliver this?

- What barriers are in your way? List them.

- How can you overcome these barriers?

- What would you do if you knew you could not fail?

The following 5 steps may help you prepare

Step 1. List your skills

If you are returning to work after an absence, think through the skills you have already acquired: list the tasks you perform on a regular basis and the skills used. Running a home demands good time, project and financial management abilities and there are many situations where you will organise and negotiate. Add any voluntary or unpaid work, for example with schools or local committees. Do be positive: take small steps initially to build your confidence. Get the support of your partner, family and relatives. Research your potential employment opportunities before undertaking extensive re-training or re-skilling.

Step 2. Translate your skills into areas of strength

Classify the skills you have identified into different groups such as people management or financial planning. From these decide which skills you most enjoy using as this may help you think about the type of work you want to do. If you have skills that are out of date or rusty then look at courses to bring them up to date, or consider some voluntary work. Review your CV and add to it – keep it up to date and it will also help remind you of your abilities.

Step 3. Identify opportunities

There are in essence five key routes to finding work:

1. agencies
2. adverts (web and newspapers, trade publications)
3. direct approaches to companies you want to work for
4. finding work through someone you know – networking
5. self-employment

You may find some easier to do than others but it is advisable to look at all. A direct approach, which is sending your CV and a covering letter to all appropriate employers, showing how you would be an asset to their company, often produces good results. For this you will need to do research and be well prepared. Think about companies and institutions that you would like to work for and apply to them directly. Have new companies moved into the area or are they likely to? Talk to everyone to get the word out that you are looking at new opportunities. The internet offers a substantial number of job sites. Use local sources of information such as libraries, directories and job centres, chambers of commerce and Business Links for example. Make use of all your networks, friends, and family, anyone who have information that may lead to opportunities as well as web based networking tools such as LinkedIn and Facebook.

Step 4. Be clear about what you are willing to do

What restrictions might you face and are they insurmountable? These could include: travel, childcare, family resistance, lack of qualifications. Work through the list and be creative in thinking how each could be overcome. What do you want to achieve by returning to work? Set some goals about your ideals. Think through hours, type of work, salary, working for yourself or with a partner. If you know what would be your "perfect" situation it can help you focus, even if you have to compromise in some areas. The first step back into employment again could be an important step towards your goal. Be realistic but don't put imaginary barriers in front of yourself.

Step 5. Draw up an action plan

Give yourself timescales and cost implications. Talk to family and friends. Seek advice. Do a business plan if needed. Keep your ultimate aim in focus and remind yourself how good it will feel when you achieve it.

Job interview preparation
8 questions to consider

1

Prepare a 30 word response to the question "Tell me about yourself". Include points you consider are unique about yourself.

2

What are my core skills and experience?

3

What attracted me to this post and organisation?

4

What achievements will the interviewer be most interested in?

5

What can I deliver for my next employer?

6

What possible problem areas are there in my application and how can I address them positively?

7

What lasting impression do I want to leave with my interviewer?

8

After the interview – what have I learned?

Personal Story

We talked to a legal professional returning to work after ten years as a stay-at-home mother. These are her responses to our questions.

What were your chief worries about returning to work?

Whether I'd be able to do the job and manage the juggling act. I worried about my lack of confidence and feeling out of touch.

Were those worries warranted?

Actually doing the job was fine and I was easily able to get back in the swing. I discovered I had acquired other skills while not at work.

What was most helpful to you?

My colleagues – they freely gave me practical support.

What advice did you find most helpful?

Not taking on too many hours proved helpful. Negotiating terms properly was essential right from the beginning. Be careful what you commit to.

Make sure you have the back-up such as cleaning, walking the dog. If you can afford it, pay for help.

What impact has it had on your family life?

There has been no difference in terms of friends, although I've had less social life. I'm no longer physically able to be there for school activities etc. I'm unable to be at some school functions for children but have to accommodate that. We ensure the other parent is there if possible.

No longer able to indulge myself but must now prioritise. The children seem oblivious to the changes. In holidays more organisation is required but as the children are older now they appreciate being cared for by older teenagers. It's much more fun for them! The impact on me was the realisation that I like to be in control and still struggle to ensure the control is still there. There is an anxiety about still wanting to do everything as I used to. Less control means not being on top of things. For example there are no more clear days to sort the house etc. My husband appears to consider nothing has changed.

Was it the right decision for you?

I'm enjoying the work and the money it brings. There has been a huge cultural change in the workplace which I've had to get used to. When life throws something unexpected at you such as a bereavement, then the juggling becomes even more stressful.

What have been the benefits?

I've enjoyed making more of an effort with dressing for work. I feel more confident. I feel I have my own identity and a sense of achievement. There are guilt-free gifts for children. and it is encouraging greater independence in them.

What have been the reactions of others?

Colleagues say they have benefited by having me there as it has reduced their pressure. Some friends are curious about my change in lifestyle. They found it hard to understand or felt guilty they weren't doing the same.

If you could change anything, what would it be?

To have reduced travelling time and to work only two days per week.

How did you prepare to return?

Actually I was too frightened to prepare too much as I was in denial about returning. I did do a bit by reading some documents etc. and had some help with IT skills. I increased cleaners' hours to prepare the home.

I wished there had been time to sort the house out prior to returning.

Anything to add?

I still worry about being in control and not having time for myself. This can feel oppressive. I need to say 'no' more often. I no longer have time to read books.

To sum up, what would be your top tips?

Before starting a job put a framework in place to help you with running the house and coping with the children. Buy in help in the form of cleaners / dog walkers. Accept offers of help from friends and family. Learn to ask for help – there will always be a time when you can repay the favour. If you have a chance to renegotiate your hours, do not over extend yourself. Commit to less rather than more, you can always ask to increase your hours, in the future. (I realise not everyone will have the choice.) Try not to do everything once you start work, accept that some things will have to change. Don't feel guilty about not attending every school function. Learn to say 'no'. You can't do it all! Raise your expectations of your spouse and children — after all they are getting financial benefits. Encourage them to take on more responsibility.

In the workplace have confidence in your ability, especially if you are returning to a similar job — it took me three weeks maximum to feel that I had never been away. Do take every training opportunity (especially in IT if your skills are lacking), even if you don't think it is strictly relevant. Don't be afraid to ask colleagues for help. Mine have been great without exception. Returning to work will:

> Bring a sense of achievement.

> Help you regain a sense of identity.

> Give you an excuse to buy some new clothes and encourage you to make more effort with your appearance.

> Improve your confidence.

> Make sure you spend your time off wisely and become more disciplined with your time.

> Lastly, practise what you preach!

Chapter Five

Working from Home

"I work for myself, which is fun. Except when I call in sick, I know I'm lying."

Rita Rudner

There's been quite a trend in the past few years for an increase in the number of people working from home and the improvements in technology have made it all the more possible. Is this something you have thought about? Would it work for you? Is this an option for your kind of employment or are you thinking about working for yourself? To help you make your mind up, we begin this chapter with a table of pros and cons and follow up with lots of tips should you decide that working from home would suit you.

Working from home: why do it?

"I like being President. The pay is good and I can walk to work"

John F. Kennedy

Advantages	Disadvantages	Other Considerations
Greater flexibility in managing work / home balance.	It can be hard to stop as the hours you work are up to you.	How much of a perfectionist are you? Will you find it hard if there is no one to tell you to stop work/turn off the office lights? How easily are you distracted?
Reduced or no commuting travel time to place of work.	Commuting can be useful for 'getting rid of the day', dealing with admin, learning something new, reading.	Is having a place of work separate from your home important to you?
Reduced stress being in your own home environment.	There is a risk you feel you are always 'at work' and boundaries can be hard to define.	Does the nature of your work lend itself to working from home? Conference calls abroad are technically achievable but if your children are being cared for in the home, will this work?

Working From Home

Advantages	Disadvantages	Other Considerations
Reduced cost of travel, car-parking, clothes, food.	Increased costs in the home for utilities and possible extra costs for technology, equipment and training.	How will it be if you take over living space for your work?
Greater contact with children.	Can be confusing for family members who may want your attention yet you are technically 'at work'.	How well will it fit in with the ages of your children and your current childcare arrangements?
Can give greater autonomy over time, as there are no closing hours to your place of work. Your work can fit in with your family life more easily.	Can lead to over-working or even burn-out.	Could you work from home for a specific period of time? It doesn't have to be a lifetime decision.
You have the opportunity to pop the washing on, be there for a delivery or service engineers and others.	The perceptions of others that you are not really at work and can break off to do other things – or that you don't have a 'proper job'.	Could you have times when you are "unavailable" during the day and communicate this?
Increased productivity as there is likely to be less disruption and better quality thinking time.	Lack of productivity if you are easily distracted or lack self-motivation.	Have you considered the nature of the work you do as well as your personality type in making your decision?

Advantages	Disadvantages	Other Considerations
May give you the opportunity to set up your own business from home.	Can be lonely. You can lose the benefits of working in a team, having the support of and the opportunities for bouncing ideas off others.	Do you prefer working alone or working in a team the majority of the time? There won't be a built-in structure to call upon and therefore you will need to be more self-sufficient and resourceful.
You avoid workplace politics.	Can be excluded from what's happening in the main workplace.	Is your promotion influenced by your visibility in the work place? How good are the communications to help keep you in touch?
Can increase your knowledge and skills as you need to be more self-sufficient in areas such as IT skills, employment and self-employment.	There is little opportunity to learn from others and have your training paid for.	Is learning new skills important to you and if so, will you be able to do this if you are working from home?

1. Preparation for working from home

The 6 key steps

1. Decision. Decide if this would suit you, your family, your employer, the nature of your work and your home environment. The table on the previous pages may help with your decision. Without an honest appraisal of these factors there may be a temptation to believe working from home could be an easy solution to current frustrations. This may be so, however, it brings its own difficulties.

2. Options. Having decided to work from home, there are two key options. One is that you resign your current post and set up in business for yourself. There are books and websites that may help with this and some are referenced in Appendices C and D. The second option is that you negotiate working from home with your current employer. If it is the latter, it will be worth considering your proposal from your employer's perspective. What might be the benefits to him or her? For instance, might it help reduce the company's overheads or increase productivity? Some employers might welcome this so it's worth asking. Consider how you will ensure you are always up to date if you are not in the shared workplace. It may be possible for you to ask for a trial period to see how it works for all parties.

3. Childcare. Before your children are at school, plan childcare. It is unfair to your employer and/or yourself to try to work and look after your children at the same time. Babies seem to need you just when you have organised that conference call to the US!

4. Home. Think about where in your home you will work. What will suit you, the family and your work best? A converted box room, a tailor made study, the laptop on your kitchen table or even a more adventurous solution such as building a log cabin in the garden or converting a garage? It probably depends upon you and what kind of work you are doing. It may help to base yourself in different parts of the house depending on the task - writing, researching, dealing with calls or administration.

5. Equipment. Make sure you have the right environment and equipment to carry out your work such as a dedicated phone line, filing cabinet, computer technology if required, good lighting and a place to be quiet and if possible leave work out until the next day.

6. Administration. If you elect to work for yourself, don't forget the administration you'll need for becoming self-employed. These include informing the Inland Revenue, paying your N.I., ensuring you submit a tax return and pay any necessary tax by the end of January each year, taking out personal and public liability insurance for yourself and your home, keeping accurate invoices and financial records including receipts. For some a VAT return will be necessary.

"In the UK, more than a third of female entrepreneurs are aged thirty or under, and 74% of women who started a business did so before their child was 2."

Lydia Slater, Sunday Times Style magazine, 2008

10 tips for making it work

To manage working from home needs a bit of thinking through. The trick is to get the most from the benefits and minimise the drawbacks.

1.

Even if working from home means you don't come face to face with people, you may still need to have a professional persona. Little things can help to set the tone. For example you might continue to dress as if in an office, or think about the difference your body posture can make when you're on the phone. The key is to know what works for you.

2

Working in isolation can mean that the usual structures, rewards and feedback may no longer be there. Consider what you need to motivate yourself and try different ways. It might be regular breaks, a variety of tasks, some company, deadlines or targets achieved and even asking for feedback from those you respect and trust.

3

It's easy to continue working all hours just because you can. Avoid spending all night on the computer or on that project.

4

As mentioned previously, one benefit of working from home is that you can get ahead with the washing or some cooking. However, choosing to do something domestic in the house can also be a distraction. If the distraction enables you to work through an issue and give you some useful thinking time then go ahead. However, be honest and find your own way to keep on track.

5

A huge benefit of working for yourself, if you give yourself permission to do this, is to be confident about taking time out for you and the children. All you need to say is "I'm unavailable that day" as no-one will know if you are with another client or attending sports day!

6.

Working from home alone for a continuous period can be very hard. If your work allows it, break up your days at home with meetings. If it doesn't, then plan to do errands, see or call friends to help punctuate your work.

7

Procrastination and time wasting robs precious minutes, even hours, from us all, but particularly when you work from home. This can be a huge issue. You can spend hours 'perfecting' a task or avoiding starting one. Recognise when this is happening and develop techniques to get out of it! Set the alarm on your mobile?

8

Manage your phone calls. Do you want to let people know when you prefer to receive calls whether business or personal? Do you have international clients who will be on a different time zone?

9

Build in time to market yourself and find new work.

10

Think about the difference between working alone and working in a team when it comes to managing your workload. Working for five clients one day a week is very different from working for the same client or company five days a week. It may be that you need to buy in some additional support such as administration, accounts, sales calls or even a virtual PA.

Many thanks to Pam Truman for her contribution to this section.

You may also find the following questions useful to help manage your workload.

Ask yourself

1. Does it need to be done? If yes, can it be done by someone else? If so, who?

2. Is this is the best use of my time?

3. Am I doing too much?

4. Is what I have done good enough?

5. Is my deadline realistic?

Personal Story

I found that trying to get ready for my next client at the end of each working day was just too much and so I employed a dear friend who helped keep me sane. Gill organised my work on a part time basis, kept my invoices up to date and did all the admin work so I could be out earning.

Wendy

Expressing yourself assertively

Some people view the fact that you work from home

 as "not really being at work" and don't understand that you aren't available for coffee / shopping / errands. Here are some responses to possible situations.

Perceived criticism about not running an errand for your partner:

"Like you, I've been working today and it hasn't been possible. I have time to do it at the end of the week, if I've completed the job."

Friend / neighbour – "You're not doing anything tomorrow are you?"

"Yes, I am at work and will be locked away in my office".

Plumber etc. who wants to talk:

"I have a business call that I need to make in five minutes".

Child asking you to play:

"I need to finish this bit of work first and then I'd love to in half an hour."

Carer wants to chat:

"I must get on. Can we talk later?"

Telephone calls:

"I'm working on something at the moment. Can we speak later?"

Employers perspective: 2 considerations

1

Communicate to your employer about your expected working patterns so there is no misunderstanding regarding your availability. For example, you may need to do something with the children during typical working hours. Be open about this and reassure your employer or colleagues that your work will be done at a different time.

2

Working from home means that people won't see the difficulties that you might face, so it is even more important to keep to deadlines and deliver what you have promised or explain when you can't.

2 ideas for looking after yourself

1

Take time out for a proper lunch break or a walk. You will be much more productive as a result.

2

Health & Safety is a consideration even when working from home for you and any visitors. Is your furniture fit for purpose? Are you safe and comfortable working from home? What legal implications are relevant for the type of business you are operating? Contact the

Health and Safety Executive for advice and information at www.hse.gov.uk

Self-employment – 8 tips for getting organised

1

If you work for more than one client, keep one diary to avoid double booking.

2

Establish your fee structure at the start of the relationship with a client so that they know in advance what your terms are. What happens if you have allocated time to them, giving up other clients and then they cancel? A sliding scale of cancellation charges is useful.

3

Get good advice on what you can claim for when working from home. You may find it more economical to use a bookkeeper for your accounts and then an accountant only once a year to sign off the accounts. If you manage your own accounts be meticulous and keep your records for seven years in case the tax people come to call.

4

Organisation at home is very important. Keep a file for all your invoices, statements and receipts for the year. Write on the front of your cheque book the dates of the first and last cheque so you can easily access them. Ensure you write the relevant invoice information on the paying-in stub too.

5

Keep work receipts on a spike and make it a habit to empty your bag and purse at the end of the day or week. Each month transfer these to a dated envelope and file.

6

A separate bank account for work is essential and it may be helpful to meet with your nearest branch to set up all you need. Some offer support and advice and free banking for a peiod.

7

Administration, developing new work, learning new skills, keeping accounts, chasing invoices, acquiring keyboard skills, all have to be built into your new way of working. It can be too easy to regard this as periphery work and only think of the more obvious "paid" aspects as the real work. It all needs doing well though and your salary or daily rate needs to cover this time. Don't forget to include preparation time. Keep an eye on market rates and consider what your client(s) can afford, but don't undersell yourself.

8

Invoice management. Many people pay late so if you are organised you can keep on top of it. Present your invoice on completion of the work to keep delays to a minimum. Keep accurate records. If you find it difficult to chase people for payment, ask someone else to do it on your behalf. This can be a professional arrangement or ask a friend to be your "accounts manager" chasing your bills. In this way you can keep your relationship with your client separate. Your time and expertise is worth something, so don't be afraid to ask for what has been agreed. Put your payment terms on each invoice such as "Payment due within 21 days".

4 tips on sharing your workspace and home

1

Don't spread out so much that everywhere you and others look, there is work!

2

Try to keep workspace separate from family space and close that space at the end of the working day if you can.

3

Discuss the sharing of the computer and phone with your children and partner. Can you establish times and turns? Negotiating to avoid conflict is important here if you need to share equipment but do be flexible about accommodating forgotten homework or urgent emails.

4

Learn to ignore arguments that go on in your house. If you weren't there they would have to sort them out without you.

5 thoughts on tools and technology

1

Gadgets, tools and technology. What do you need, where does it need to be and how will it be maintained and serviced? For some people, organising this to begin with will be very important such as having a gadget to synchronise several diaries. For others it may be better to see what you need as you and your business develops.

2

The internet can be a deadly distraction. One of our friends found she was doing a 'quick search' for cheap flights when she was supposed to be working, which developed into organising a full blown weekend away! Instant messaging can be a similar distraction. Only activate those applications you need for the task in hand. So, for example, if a report needs completion turn off the instant messaging, internet and inbox facilities to allow you to concentrate.

3

Caller ID or excluding cold callers can prevent a huge amount of wasted time and importantly stop your thought process from being interrupted. Contact your telephone provider for these services.

4

Have back up contingency plans to ensure you don't lose vital documents on your computer and make sure hard copies are stored safely too.

5

Protect your own and your business information and intellectual property by using a shredder or other secure destruction service.

4 thoughts from the children's perspective

1

Help children to distinguish between their parent "at work" and parent "not at work" and understand how it affects them.

2

Be fair with what you expect of your child when you are working from home – if you are on a conference call is it reasonable to expect them to be silent? To stop singing for example? Explain what your needs are and then make appropriate arrangements such as organising for them to be taken for a walk.

3

Replicating a working space for your child/children can help them feel included and also establishes a pattern for homework and personal study for the future.

4

Children love knowing where you work and what you do. We found taking our children into our offices or school left a lasting impression on them. Working from home is different but it can still be explained as being a special place. Involving them occasionally in what we do is mutually beneficial, whether it is little ones putting stamps on envelopes or the older ones making a more substantial contribution, such as Penny's sons helping her prepare her school assemblies.

5 child care tips

1

As your children grow up you may decide to manage without childcare but be aware it seems that children need help with homework or their love lives just when you have a difficult telephone call to make! Have clear rules about when you can be interrupted. Maybe something like: if the office door is open they can come in, if it is closed – no entry.

2

If you have childcare provision at home, be very clear with the children and nanny or au pair about who they should turn to. Children may well try and come to you if they don't get the answer they were hoping for from their carer. Undermining others because you happen to be there is a dangerous thing.

3

It's courteous to respect your child care provider's hours. If you are in the house then it may or may not be ok for you to carry on with something that you want to finish – just check it out and negotiate what is acceptable to both of you.

4

It may be possible to offer your current childcare provider some additional paid tasks to help you in your work. They earn some extra money, gain an understanding of your work, feel trusted by you to do a good job, and you may be advised by your accountant that you can claim some of the costs.

5

Be aware that the person looking after you child may feel more self-conscious having you in the house. It may inhibit the type of activities they want to organise for the children because of the possible noise. They may feel awkward tackling discipline. Be sensitive to this and talk it through. If you need quiet for a period, suggest they organise an outing or some outside play.

Personal Story

"The situation of a freelance writer is untypical, because you don't have the imperative of 'the office', a sort of offstage 'she who must be obeyed'. It can be more difficult to shut yourself away behind a closed door and a busy sign, because you are saying 'No-one else is making me do this; I'm doing it because I want to.'

When my children were young I worked on the mornings the youngest was at playgroup and on Saturdays when their wonderful father took over for the whole day. I learned to close my ears to all oaths, imprecations, tantrums and tears - their dad had to deal with it.

Working at home, its essential to put the work first, that is to say before other tasks. For me, getting up early is essential because it's peaceful and the rest of the world is still stewing in its pit. By the time 9 am comes round, the phone starts ringing, family and friends start calling and life generally hammers on the door, at least I'll have done something. And on quiet days the impetus of a good start can carry me through.

A system of rewards is essential, and then one can bring deferred gratification into play, e.g. 'I shall have a coffee but only when I've turned the next page.' I find it helpful to operate on an extremely short-term basis. A novel is such a huge enterprise that there's a danger of inertia panic setting in. I break the whole exercise down into small manageable chunks.

Everyone has a low-wattage time of day. Mine's the afternoon. (Dorothy Parker said there was only one thing afternoons were good for and it was seldom available to the working girl...but that's by the by) I can put in plenty of hours between 5 or 6 am and 1 pm and perhaps a little more in the late afternoon/ early evening. Once I recognised that and gave in to it went a long way to banishing guilt - and guilt is the enemy of creativity (and so much else besides)

With three grandchildren living locally it would be awfully easy to become hot-and-cold-running-babysitting. I love to see them, but find it's best to put arrangements in place to suit all of us rather than simply 'be available'.

Oh, one more thing - have a dog. It has to be walked, and that's a terrific reason to take a break as well as being mentally and physically therapeutic.

Good luck with your great idea.(For the book, 'Spinning Plates')

Sarah x"

Sarah Harrison,

Author of numerous books including "The Dreaming Stones", "Flowers of the Field" and "How to write a Blockbuster".

Personal Story

Penny and I had decided to work on this chapter and had a few hours one afternoon together. Penny was nervously awaiting a bank transfer to go through so we decided to walk from my house to my very nearby village to get a sandwich so she could "walk off" her anxiety. We felt with this break and a catch-up we could then be very focused and make the most of our few brief hours together. Well, readers, let me tell you it illustrated the benefits and disadvantages of working from home beautifully — so much so Penny made a record of all that happened that afternoon.

A beautiful October afternoon, unusually sunny, we sat on the pavement eating our sandwiches — well on chairs next to a table on the pavement, (we leave sitting on the pavement to the neighbourhood teenagers).

I saw a woman that I needed to have a conversation with so grasped the opportunity — great — saved me several attempts trying to find her number, not getting hold of her etc. We went to the Post Office to get ourselves ready for sending off our synopsis and chapters to agents but there was a postal strike so we couldn't get very far. On the way home my son, who had just gone to University a couple of weeks ago rang to ask how he should wash a jumper ("Read what's on it", says I — "Nike" he said — no, not really). I feel guilty I haven't told him all there is to know about washing his clothes but feel great he calls for a quick chat and finishes with "love you loads".

We get home and my other son arrives home from school hoping for a chat but doesn't get one as Penny and I need to work. He then goes off to rugby. When he gets there he realises he has left some kit and could I get it for him and bring it up. My daughter rings asking for a lift home from school (she normally walks) as her friend has hurt her ankle. Penny then gets a call from one of her sons asking it she can help with transport that night and her other son calls to say he is back in the country. Penny then gets a call to say her money transfer has gone through successfully. My doorbell goes and it's my neighbour wanting to talk. Oh! and he tells me off for not having remembered to put the recycling bins out!

By the time I get back to Penny she is in hysterics as, at this point, we have barely done a thing and we need to finish soon!

Penny can't drink from her glass of water as its cracked and I then get a work call and have to respond urgently to an email (this is my day off, of course).

Jess calls asking why I've taken so long to pick her up and then Ted does the same about the whereabouts of his kit!

Penny needs to leave to pick up the car before the garage closes,

I have 2 trips to help the children out and the chapter still isn't finished!

We realised that we allow ourselves to become involved in so many other aspects of life when working from home — and this can be a great blessing and a great distraction! We have yet to watch daytime TV!

Wendy

Chapter Six

Managing Yourself and Your Home: Spinning the Time Plate

"Things which matter most should never be at the mercy of things that matter least!"

Goethe

"If only I had more time." How often have we heard that phrase, especially by working mothers? We all have the same amount of time available to us and, although hard at times, deciding how to spend it is actually up to us. What do you want more time for? Would it be for family, work and career development, friends, health and fitness, personal and spiritual growth, home life, relaxation and fun or even sleep! In this chapter we look at ways to manage yourself so that you can find some precious time for those things you want or need to do. We cover a whole range of ideas and tips, some of which may appear contradictory, as we appreciate that what will suit some of you, may not suit others. Knowing what works for you and what barriers you face, will help you understand which of these to try.

Managing yourself

The topics of conversation during the first five years of the working mums' group we belonged to focused heavily on the needs of the child. It gradually dawned on us that we needed to look after ourselves too and if we were to spin those plates we had to be a little more selfish and make time for ourselves. Building some time for fun, exercise, quiet time away from the family, can be just what your mind and body need to reenergize and invigorate you and to help you cope with the more challenging times.

10 tips that help

1

Make sure you have some 'me' time each day; even a quarter of an hour will make you even more productive later on. When you feel good/happy/productive, remember the details so you can recapture the feelings. Store these in your memory to call upon when needed. Use all your senses when creating your "me" time: be aware of your surroundings, use a scented candle or some favourite oils, notice the flavours in your food, focus on the sounds of nature or music rather than the voice and thoughts in your head. Connect with your surroundings, take some deep breaths and allow yourself to relax. Enjoy your time.

2

Notice when you work best and have the most energy so that demanding tasks can be done at these times rather than when your energy drops. For example, if you are a morning person, get up really early and have work completed by the time children are up and needing attention.

3

Book an early appointment with your hairdresser so you are seen before they fall behind. Book your next appointment before you leave. Some hairdressers can organise for you to have your nails done at the same time as you are having your hair done.

4

Carry spare items in your bag such as make-up, tights and toothbrush. If you travel a lot, have a second set of toiletries and make-up ready for packing.

5

Have handbags with lots of compartments for specific items such as mobile phone, keys and lipstick to avoid having to waste time searching for them. Alternatively, use a bag liner with all the essentials in. Popping the liner into the main bag makes it is easier when you swap handbags.

6

Clear plastic shoeboxes are ideal for storing accessories as you can see what you are looking for at a glance.

7

Don't bother to arrive early for any medical appointments. It's highly unlikely you'll be seen ahead of time.

8

"I've got fast grooming down to a fine art. I have my eyelashes tinted, take baths wearing a three-minute face mask and use a foundation that lasts all day" says Julia Carling, co-author of "Beauty Scoop: The Indispensable Guide to the Best Beauty Products on the Market"

9

Plan for the next day by choosing your clothes, getting food out of the freezer and putting anything needed for school by the door ready to pick up.

10

Say "No". Have you thought about your own limits and boundaries when it comes to giving time and attention to others? This may be when friends or family or work colleagues make demands or when you think that it is your duty or responsibility. Maybe you don't call a relative as often as you or they would like but you can make it a more productive conversation if you really listen and fully engage when you do. Bad planning by someone else doesn't mean you have to react as if it is your emergency. If it doesn't get done, whose problem is it? Remember that saying "no" is about saying no to the request and not the person asking you.

16 tips for managing yourself at work

1

Check whether the task in hand is important or urgent. Sometimes the urgent stuff is someone else's agenda whereas the important things can get overlooked. Learn to say 'no' here as well as in other parts of your life.

2

Be careful about over-scheduling. Leave some free time each week and make time before and after meetings for travel, preparation, report-writing and the unexpected.

3

If possible, try to have your home, workplace and schools all within easy reach and save on that commuting time.

4

If you can't avoid commuting time, think how you can best use it. Use it for planning, reflection, personal growth, or even just 'being'. It could be an opportunity to do a little exercise such as working your stomach or pelvic floor muscles! Keep a note pad and pen with you for those great ideas that pop into your head or for writing lists.

5

Check if there are any expected delays to your travel before you set off.

6

Prioritise. Do those things which have the most impact.

7

When faced with a difficult job decide to work on it for 15 minutes. This can help you overcome the block to getting started and prevent procrastination. Often after this time the work flows.

8

If a task is likely to take less than two minutes do it straight away.

9

Handle each piece of paper only once or you could spend longer trying to find the piece of paper when you are ready to do it! The same discipline can apply to emails by filing, actioning, printing or deleting them as soon as you receive them.

10

Only open your inbox two or three times a day.

11

Estimate how long a job will take to do, give yourself a deadline and try to complete it within the allotted time. In this way you could create some much needed extra time.

12

Have a start and finish time for all meetings and social activities.

13

If you have several phone calls to make, group them together. Decide what you want to cover and achieve with each call beforehand.

14

When on the phone at home or at work, and you know you are under pressure to do another task or be somewhere else then let them know that you either can't talk to them now but could another time. Alternatively you could say that you have only a limited amount of time. This helps you to engage fully in the conversation. As you get near to the end of the time let them know you will have to close and arrange to call again if you need to.

15

Clearing your desk at the end of each day, and even more importantly at the end of your working week, helps you to feel calm and ready when approaching the next days work. However, we did spot the opposite viewpoint expressed on a desktop card stating, "A cluttered desk is a sign of genius". Just do what works for you.

16

Back up document files regularly.

Household Management

"My second favourite household chore is ironing. My first being, hitting my head on the top bunk bed until I faint!"

Erma Bombeck .

10 ideas for managing paperwork

1

Keep bills and other household correspondence in a file so that you can deal with them during commercial breaks in TV programmes.

2

Bank online. All those precious minutes you waste paying each bill could add up considerably over a year.

3

Just as in work, handle each piece of paper only once – this includes paying bills, so pay them on time or even better use direct debit.

4

Put all contact details in one folder or computer file. You can use the computer to store all addresses as labels for birthday and Christmas cards.

5

Have a list of key items on a notice board such as details of doctor, dentist, dates of children's injections and any information that you are repeatedly asked for. However, beware of leaving out documents or information that could lead to identity theft.

6

Have a list of each day's requirement for each member of the family.

7

Have a box for gifts with wrapping paper, ribbons, cards and tape all ready to save you precious moments, at Christmas or when a birthday is due.

8

Encourage family members to write down things you might be running short of on a notepad or blackboard. These can then be added to the shopping list.

9

Save time and irritation by labelling everything that needs it such as freezer containers, home videos, packs of photographs and files. This prevents defrosting a leek and potato soup only to find it was vanilla ice cream, or planning to sit down to watch a video of a family party and spending ages searching for it.

10

Stock up on the things you tend to run out of most – stamps, wrapping paper, cards, and light bulbs.

Personal Story

"I sat in bed one morning watching the low winter sun break through the window. It was a rare moment of peace, a longed for lie-in that had become virtually non-existent since my little boy was born. He is now three and that morning was helping my husband carry up a small coffee that they had made me. They passed me the cup and while I tried to nurse myself gently to face a new day after having been up three times in the night, a game of jumping began. As they laughed and jumped in concert, clouds of dust rose from the bedclothes, caught suspended in the streams of sunlight. How like my life since becoming a mum... more full of laughter than I could ever have imagined and more full of dust too. It is the dust that offends the perfectionist within me. Nothing is settled and ordered and tidy and neat and right and secure any more. Things have risen up and are exposed that I would rather have kept hidden. I am called to love, to accept and befriend in my child things that were never befriended, accepted and loved in me. It has been more painful than I ever imagined and yet I would not change it or be without him for the whole world."   *Anonymous.*

12 housework hints to help reduce stress levels

1

Invite friends round to clear clutter or help you decorate. It's much more fun that way.

2

Have a routine for cleaning, allocating specific days or times of the year for certain tasks – and stick to it.

3

Line your grill pan with foil to reduce washing up and wear and tear to the pan.

4

Set up a paper file for all information such as domestic, garden and local services plus those takeaway leaflets.

5

Decide what is important to you. Some people feel so much better if they have a swept floor or a vacuumed carpet.

6

Keep one room that you can easily have some relaxation in – even if it's the bathroom!

7

Some couples divide household tasks, such as sharing the cooking and shopping. A takeaway or a ready prepared meal can take the stress out of a very busy evening. Seek agreement on what people in the home are willing to do. You can then share out the responsibilities but suggest swapping chores after a time.

8

Clearing toys at the end of a working day can sometimes feel like the last straw. Have cupboard doors built so it can all be hidden! Keep separate labelled boxes for items such as dressing up clothes, hats and Lego. For the things left over, have another box where things can be thrown into until there is time to put them away properly. Children can be encouraged to help with this, especially if you make a game out of it.

9

Time and energy can be saved if everyone returns "things" to their designated "place". We'd love to hear how our readers manage this one!!!!

10

To manage wardrobe space, throw out something before you buy anything new.

11

Build in a monthly maintenance session for chores such as dry-cleaning, repairs, shoe heeling and cleaning the fridge.

12

To help organise laundry, you could try having two crates – one for clothes to be ironed and the other for things that don't need ironing such as socks, underwear and swimwear. One member of the family can be responsible for distributing these on a regular basis or maybe everyone just collects their own.

"I'm not going to vacuum 'til Sears makes one you can ride on".

Roseanne Barr.

Tips when paying for individual or professional services

Decide which jobs you most want to offload, such as ironing, gardening, the weekly clean or the occasional cleaning of the oven and then decide what you can afford or want to pay someone else to do.

8 things to consider when using companies for cleaning and gardening

1

Quality can vary so ask for recommendations from friends and acquaintances.

2

Although often more expensive, professional companies will normally bring all their own equipment and products and should have insurance.

3

You may be able to negotiate a discount if you give them regular work.

4

Most can be booked for specific times such as for a spring clean or you can arrange for them to have keys for regular visits.

5

Some work in a pair, which means they will be at your home for half the time.

6

Many companies have certain ways of working so it is advisable to leave clear instructions of the jobs you need doing.

7

If you have any restrictions or recommendations about certain products because of personal preferences, allergies or particular care instructions, then also make this clear.

8

Build up a relationship with someone in the company so you can give feedback on the quality of work. This is also helpful if you need to change arrangements at short notice.

12 tips regarding individual freelance cleaners and gardeners

1

Trust, of course, is the biggest issue about having someone in your home. Use "word of mouth" recommendations where possible. Good cleaners and gardeners want to have a relationship built on trust too. Ease them into the role, increasing responsibilities as the trust develops such as delaying cleaning your favourite pieces of china or replanting your favourite tree.

2

Make it clear what you will expect if something gets broken.

3

If you absolutely must have the house cleaned or the garden sorted during a particular week, let them know and consider having a backup plan in case.

4

Be aware that this may be their only source of income and if you cancel because you don't need them, they don't get paid. You may not have to pay holiday pay but you may wish to give some extra money or buy them a birthday gift to show your appreciation. If you cancel at short notice it is fairer if you pay them something, as it is highly unlikely they will be able to find other work.

5

Let them know when they are doing a good job, when something extra needs doing and if they have missed something. Friendly and honest communication will help build trust and healthy relationships. Most feel pride in their work and will get job satisfaction from making your home look good. Being respected for their work and being well-regarded can be just as important as the money and in some cases even more so. We both found that the best cleaners were those who enjoyed their work. Try to find this out at the interview stage.

6

Helping your children build appropriate and respectful relationships with your cleaners can be achieved by ensuring they do not regard them as 'slaves' or people to be used. This means that you may need a rule that an untidy bedroom won't be cleaned - it will be your children's responsibility.

7

If you have an alarm system, check that your cleaner is listed as a key holder, if this is required by your service provider. Ask your cleaners to keep keys safe and ensure they are not identifiable as belonging to your house.

8

Some individuals will be self employed which will have implications for their tax and insurance.

9

Check your household insurance to ensure you are covered for loss or breakages and in case they are injured in your home.

10

When the children were older and she had no dedicated childcare, Wendy organised for her cleaners to be in the house when the children came back from school. This meant the children didn't come into an empty house on the days she was home late from work.

11

Have a list of what you need doing when taking on a new cleaner or gardener and, if necessary, show them how you would like things done.

12

Make it clear what your expectations are in terms of breaks and accessibility to drinks. We do have a scary story about a cleaner who regularly helped herself from the drinks cabinet!

Personal Story

A wonderful cleaner of mine once rang me to rearrange her hours as she couldn't come in to do my ironing that day. I said "Not to worry, although I do have piles" and she said "Oh, they are horrible, I've got them too!"

Wendy

6 time-saving tips when shopping

1

Reduce shopping trips by buying for more than one week. Make good use of your freezer and buy extra everyday items such as toothpaste and toilet rolls.

2

Shop online for food, clothes, travel, entertainment and gifts.

3

Take advantage of Sunday morning browsing times and be ready with a full trolley when the tills open.

4

Take advantage of late night supermarket shopping when the stores are less crowded and there's no queuing.

5

Buy a week's worth of children's shirts so you don't have to wash and iron mid week.

6

If you are planning on decorating, make sure you have all the measurements of your room and that of any furniture needed, as well as swatches or details of your colour scheme, with you when you are out.

7 ways to involve children

"If your children write their names in the dust on the furniture, don't let them put the year"

Phyllis Diller.

1

Even very young children can help and start to learn organisational skills. Let them choose what they want to wear the next day and put it out ready in their room.

2

Have a dirty-washing bag or box in each bedroom and train children to put their dirty clothes in it at the end of the day. Later, show them how to use the washing machine!

3

Wendy asked for a few minutes each day of the children's time to get jobs done – sometimes it's tidying their own room or it may be helping with more general duties. If they are all doing it together it seems less onerous to the children and it stopped her having to ask more than once!

4

To help with family duties have a list of jobs such as tidying socks, setting the table, clearing the dishwasher. Sharing tasks between children and changing them around (the tasks, not the children!) every so often helps them to take responsibility. Have a rota for some of these simple activities.

5

Both Penny and Wendy expected their children to help during holidays and listed what each child was responsible for. It is your holiday too, so asking for help is reasonable.

6

When the children were younger, Wendy found that holding a "meeting" with all the family ensured the children were involved with the plans for the following week, such as travel or activities after school. Each member of the family had the opportunity to say whatever they wanted. It helped clear up any concerns that needed discussing, such as sibling arguments, use of toys and the computer, child-care arrangements and any other issues. One significant example of this was when one child asked her not to take work calls once she was home. These meetings made sure that even children as young as two had a voice.

7

Consider a car journey with children as an opportunity to talk, listen and play games. Boys especially open up more when seated next to you in a car.

"I hope my child will look back on today

And see a mother who had time to play.

There will be years for cleaning and cooking

But children grow up while we're not looking."

Commonly attributed to Ruth Hulburt Hamilton

50 reminders for stress prevention and reduction

"Being happy doesn't mean everything is perfect. It means you have decided to look beyond the imperfections."

Les Brown

Some of the suggestions below seem contradictory, but obviously they won't all apply to everyone. Some people get stressed from trying to finish everything everyday and others from not getting anything done. Your reaction to these ideas will be very personal; some will seem impossible, some difficult, some obvious and others really useful.

1

Get up 15 minutes earlier in the morning. The inevitable morning mishaps will be less stressful.

2

Prepare for the morning the evening before. Set the breakfast table. Make lunches. Put out the clothes you plan to wear.

3

Don't rely on your memory. Write down appointment times such as when to pick up the laundry or when library books are due. Keep a pad and pen by the bed to jot down anything you wish to remember the next day. "The palest pink is better than the best memory"- Old Chinese Proverb.

4

Allow 15 minutes of extra time to get to appointments. Make a commitment – for example tell your friends you will buy the wine if you are late to the restaurant!

5

Make duplicates of all keys. Bury a house key in a secret spot in the garden and carry a duplicate car key in your wallet, apart from on your key ring.

6

Practice preventative maintenance so that your car, appliances, home and relationships will be less likely to breakdown or fall apart at the worst possible moment.

7

Plan ahead. Don't let the petrol tank get below one quarter full. Keep a well stocked "emergency shelf" of provisions. Don't wait until you're down to your last postage stamp to buy more. Recharge your mobile phone regularly. Have an energy bar and fresh water (in a glass bottle) in the car.

8

Don't put up with something that doesn't work properly. If your alarm clock, wallet, shoelaces, windshield wipers - whatever - are a constant aggravation, get them fixed or get new ones.

9

If an especially unpleasant task faces you, do it early in the day and get it over with. The rest of your day will then be free of anxiety.

10

When out and planning to meet someone, discuss a contingency plan such as "If for some reason either of us is delayed, here's what we'll do ...." Or, "If we get split up in the shopping centre, here's where we'll meet." Be aware that small children may well carry out your instruction with undue haste. Penny's oldest son did this when he was pre-school. She had suggested if ever he was lost in a shop to go to one of the shop assistants for help. Within minutes of her looking at some books on the other side of an aisle, a voice over the loud speaker asked if the mother of . . . . . — yes, you've guessed!

11

Ask questions. Take a few moments to repeat back directions, or what someone expects of you.

12

Say no to extra projects, social activities and invitations you know you don't have the time or energy for. This takes practice, self-respect and a belief that everyone, everyday, needs some quiet time to relax and to be alone.

13

Unplug/turn off your phone. Do you want to take a long bath, meditate, sleep or read without interruption? Drum up the courage to temporarily disconnect. The possibility of there being a terrible emergency in the next hour or so is almost nil.

14

Turn "needs" into preferences. Our basic physical needs translate into food, water and keeping warm. Everything else is a preference. Don't get too attached to preferences.

15

Simplify, simplify, simplify.

16

Relax your standards. The world will not end if the grass doesn't get mown this weekend.

17

Make friends with non-worriers. Nothing can get you into the habit of worrying faster than associating with chronic worriers.

18

Get up and stretch every so often if your job requires that you sit for extended periods.

19

Wear earplugs. If you need to find quiet at home, pop in some earplugs.

20

Get enough sleep. If necessary use an alarm clock to remind you to go to bed.

21

Create order out of chaos. Try to organise your home and workplace so that you always know exactly where things are. Put things away where they belong and you won't have to go through the stress of losing things.

22

When feeling stressed, most people tend to breathe in short, shallow breaths. When you breathe like this, stale air is not expelled, oxidation of the tissues is incomplete and muscle tension frequently results. Check your breathing throughout the day and before, during and after high pressure situations. If you find your stomach muscles are knotted and your breathing is shallow, relax all your muscles and take several deep, slow breaths. Note how, when you're relaxed both your abdomen and chest expand when you breathe. Try the following yoga technique whenever you feel the need to relax. Inhale deeply through your nose to the count of 8. Then, exhale very slowly through your mouth to the count of 16, or as long as you can. Concentrate on the long sighing sound and feel the tension dissolve. Repeat 10 times.

23

Writing your thoughts and feelings down (in a journal or on paper to be thrown away) can help you clarify things and give you a renewed perspective. Deal with a situation before it becomes a crisis.

24

Be prepared to wait. A paperback can make a wait in a queue almost pleasant.

25

Become more flexible. Not everything has to be done perfectly.

26

Get rid of destructive self talk such as "I'm too old to.....", "I'm too fat to...."

27

Use your weekend time for a change of pace. If your working week is slow and patterned, make sure there is action and time for spontaneity built into your weekends. If your working week is fast-paced and full of people and deadlines, seek peace and solitude during your days off. Feel as if you aren't accomplishing anything tangible at work? Tackle a job at the weekend that you finish to your satisfaction.

28

"Worry about the pennies and the pounds will take care of themselves". That's another way of saying; take care of today as best you can and yesterday and tomorrow will take care of themselves.

29

Do one thing at a time. When you are with someone, be with that person and with no one or anything else. When you are busy with a project, concentrate on doing just that.

30

Every day do something you really enjoy.

31

Schedule a realistic day. Avoid the tendency to arrange back-to-back appointments, allowing time between appointments for a breathing spell.

32

When the stress of having to get a job done gets in the way of getting the job done, a diversion such as a change in activity and/or your environment may be just what you need.

33

Talk it out. Discussing your problems with a trusted friend can help clear your mind of confusion so you can concentrate on solutions.

34

Learn to live one day at a time.

35

Save information regularly. Back up your PC. Store phone numbers on your PC as well as on your mobile phone. Photocopy passports and important documents and leave a set with family or friends. Consider sending yourself a disguised email containing important information such as passport numbers and insurance details that you can access remotely.

Photograph your best pieces of jewellery in case they are lost or stolen.

36

Take a hot bath or shower, or a cool one in the summer to relieve tension.

37

Do something for somebody else.

38

Focus on understanding rather than on being understood, on loving rather than on being loved.

39

Do something that will improve your appearance. Looking better can help you feel better.

40

Learn to delegate responsibility to capable others.

41

Don't forget to take a lunch break. Try to get away from your desk or work area in body and mind, even if it's just for 15 or 20 minutes.

42

Forget about counting to 10. Count to 1000 before doing something or saying anything that could make matters worse.

43

Have a forgiving view of events and people. Accept the fact that we live in an imperfect world.

44

Have an optimistic view of the world. Believe that most people are doing the best they can.

45

Do nothing, which, after being done, leads you to tell a lie.

46

Review your diet and exercise schedule.

47

Make use of meditation and/or relaxation tapes, CDs and downloads.

48

At times of stress or when you're feeling low, a really helpful technique that we have used is to write down at nighttime three positive experiences from the day. Alternatively this can be done at the start of the day when you write down three things you feel grateful for. There might be days when it can be a struggle to find something but searching can affect the way you view life. Some examples of our positive reflections, even when times were tough; driving home safely, the scent of a flower, a cuddle from a child.

49

Remember a time when you have felt calm and confident and recall as many details as possible. Practise this technique and use it whenever you feel the need to reduce your stress levels.

50

For every one thing that goes wrong, there are probably 10 or 50 or 100 blessings. Count them!

Miscellaneous – 14 more ideas

1

Check in online when flying to avoid extra waiting time at the airport. Some airlines allow you to check in well ahead of the flight time so do find out.

2

Lists, lists and more lists ensure you don't forget things. Jot things down as they come into your head then you can forget them. Keep a small notebook or pad with you at all times.

3

If lists don't work for you then try a daily action plan. Restrict yourself to the two key daily priorities that are achievable then other items won't be a distraction.

4

Ask yourself, "Does it have to be me?" and delegate where possible, either to a work colleague, another member of the family or by paying someone else.

5

If frost is expected and your car is outside, cover the windscreen with an old blanket or newspaper to save scraping time in the morning.

6

Record your favourite TV programmes, especially those on commercial channels, then you can fast-forward through the advertisements

7

Don't be afraid to ask for help from your network of friends who may be experts in different fields from you. Swapping skills and knowledge can save both money and time.

8

When booking a table at a restaurant, book it for 10 or 15 minutes before the hour so that your order is on its way when others are just arriving for their 'on-the-hour' reservation.

9

Using timers for how long a task should take, helps focus the mind and gives a sense of achievement when the task is completed on time. Using them with children can add a sense of fun to getting something done.

10

Have a plan but also the flexibility to respond to changes. For example if your washing machine breaks down, do you know a good friend or laundry service that will tide you over? If your car goes for a service, what will you do for transport if it needs additional work?

11

If you are disorganised try and work out why. Is it a lack of assertiveness and you struggle to say no to things and end up doing too much? Is it an inability to prioritise or delegate? If you can work out why then you can learn how to do things differently through practice or by asking for help from colleagues, friends or family members

12

Can you make it fun? For instance, if a cupboard or the spare room is so full of junk that it is causing you stress, turn clearing out and organising it into a pleasure. Invite a friend to help, play music and promise a glass of wine when the job's done.

13

If you find you are not completing tasks that you have set yourself, consider changing the way or time that you tackle them. Look for ways to make it more interesting, such as doing bills with a coffee on a Saturday morning rather than late at night.

14

Be wary of being a perfectionist and ask yourself "is this good enough?" or "is going the extra mile worth the pay off?" What is the impact if you do something without it having to be perfect?

If you could only have the second one first...

First Child	Second Child
Read poetry and play classical music to the bump.	Peace and quiet would be good!
Designer baby clothes.	Second-hand shop & hand-me-downs.
Weigh baby daily.	Guess by squeezing a leg occasionally.
One spot on the bottom— visit the GP.	Nappy rash – cover it up.
Sterilise all equipment.	Eats off floor.
Shown off to visitors.	What visitors?
Nappies changed constantly.	See nappy rash!
Long walks in the fresh air.	Pram by open window.
"He was born at 12 minutes past 10."	"I think it was July the something.""
Photo every expression.	Anyone seen the camera?
Completed baby book.	Blank pages.
"Sshh, was that the baby?"	I'll go up later.

First Child	Second Child
Drive around at night to get baby to sleep.	Watch TV.
Don't let him out of your sight.	Comes home when he's hungry.
Look forward eagerly to their next stage.	Wish you could hold back time.
Organic home cooked pureed vegetables.	Hope she likes left-overs.
Colour co-ordinated all new wardrobe.	Turn it inside out on the third day.
Keep every drawing and scribble.	Will wait for something to sell.

Adapted (by us) from an original idea from the Dallas Association for Parent Education Inc.

14 tips to help when feeding the family

"For 30 years my mother served us nothing but leftovers. The original meal has never been found!"

Calvin Trillin

1

Whiz up a load of garlic when fresh and store in a small jar of olive oil. This ensures you always have fresh garlic without the hassle. Approximately one teaspoon equals a clove. Some retailers have a range of this kind of fresh herbs and spices.

2

The following are perfect for keeping in your store cupboard: tinned tuna; vegetables in oil for pasta sauces; good quality pasta sauces: tinned tomatoes or passata; tomato, chilli and curry pastes; pulses and stock. In the fridge or freezer, store bagged salads, custard, smoked fish; pastry; frozen fruit and vegetables. Store herbs in the freezer once you've used what you need. When storing vegetables, they are best kept in a container lined with kitchen roll and put in the fridge rather than in their original wrapping.

3

Collect some quick and easy recipes before the baby arrives in preparation for when you have less time.

4

Many children have phases of being fussy eaters. Reassuringly, small children won't go hungry for long. If the fussy eater is a baby, just let them wait for the next meal; if older then perhaps they can assist with the meal by helping to shop and prepare the food with you. They could even start to grow their own vegetables, have their own cookery book made from recipes they have helped with. Offer them smaller portions or let them serve their own food. Children often eat a wider range of food at other people's homes or restaurants.

5

If you need to make a different meal for your children from the rest of the family, a mini-roast works well. A small piece of chicken or red meat, with a couple of potatoes can be roasted in the oven in one dish, quickly and simply and then served with a vegetable.

6

Freeze small portions of food in ice-cube trays for babies.

7

Slow cookers can be great for having a meal ready at the end of the day if time is short. There is no need to fry anything first, simply throw meat and vegetables into the cooker and then the meal will be ready when you return. If doing a curry, add the rice to the cooker on your return from work, which takes about 20 minutes. Just think, only one pot for clearing up!

8

During the week make good use of one-pot recipes, even if you don't use a slow cook pot, to save on time and kitchen mess.

9

Rice cookers are another good timesaving buy.

10

If your children enjoy mashed potatoes but reject other vegetables, try adding some carrots or leeks to the mash. It helps to cook them a little first for about five minutes before mixing in with the potatoes.

11

Add some cheese and leeks to balls of stuffing to ensure they are a little healthier and add more vegetables than meat when making a shepherd's pie or a spaghetti bolognese.

12

Have two or three recipes that are stress free and quick to make if needed in a hurry, such as something from the freezer or an easily assembled cold meat salad.

13

Set the table before you start cooking as it signals that food is on the way and somehow makes the wait seem shorter. Have a healthy snack available for when the family get in. This can help keep blood sugar levels up and irritability levels down!

14

Have all your utensils and ingredients to hand before you start cooking.

For 17 tried and tested recipes for easy family meals see Appendix F.

"Kids will eat anything — snot, scabs, soil, earwax, toenail clippings. But not sprouts."

Tony Burgess.

"In general my children refuse to eat anything that hasn't danced on television"

Erma Brombeck

A Mum's Tale

"So, what have you done today?" Thinking "not much really", I reflected on what had I done, given this was in theory mostly a day off? All I had to do today was meet with Penny, go to Pilates, meet a client and write 6 reports. Ok, I dropped my daughter and her friends at school, went to bank to get money for the cleaner, but the cash point wasn't working. My friend needed a lift to collect her car. I was due to be working on the book with Penny first thing but my car had a flat tyre again and I needed to get the newly ordered one put on. Garage was due to ring when new tyre came in. Called them twice to chase. Went to garage and of course they found more problems so had to wait. Took dog for a walk/run/drag. Went to Pilates. (Can you relax whilst in a hurry and thinking "I should really be at home writing up reports and seeing Penny and doing other stuff" and still BREATHE and relax? Mmm didn't think so.) Went back to cash point to get money. Said hello to cleaner whilst running around tidying up so she could at least see the surfaces to clean. Got changed to go to client meeting. Made it with a minute to spare. Finished meeting. Came back and pulled onto drive as Penny arrived for our rearranged meeting. Worked on book. Managed to raise a smile from cross teenager who had to walk home from school as I wasn't free

to pick her up (Why? What else have you been doing...?).
Answered telephone to a wrong number. Wrote thank you
note to friends for dinner at weekend and delivered it.
Received text from son urgent document to be sent to him.
Rang mother-in-law to check on her. Neil's train was late
home, went to pick him up from station. Answered a cold
call. Made dinner. Helped daughter with homework. Patted
dog. Checked emails. Wrote this. Went off to dance class,
came back, emptied dishwasher again, hung up washing, sent
text to other son and got stuff ready for work tomorrow — and
it's only Monday (and I still haven't written my
reports....)!"   Wendy.

Spinning Plates

Chapter Seven

Building Children's Self Esteem and Independence

"Children will not remember you for the material things you provided for them but for the feeling that you cherished them."

Richard L. Evans

Why this chapter? A common fear amongst working parents is that they are damaging their child in some way by not spending enough time with them. Our belief is that how you spend your time with your children is as important, if not more so, than the amount. Given that you may have limited time, this chapter helps to focus on the key ways in which you can help your children develop their self-esteem and grow to be independent adults. Don't forget the benefits that being a working parent can bring to our children that we may not always appreciate, particularly around issues of independence.

My Rights (as a child)

I have a right to:

Ask for what I want   - even though people might say 'no'

Ask for help   -   even if people seem too busy or don't want to help

Have ideas   -   even if people think they are silly

Feel my feelings — even when people say I shouldn't have those feelings

Make mistakes - especially when I've tried my very best

Try and try again — even if some people may think I can't do it

Change my mind sometimes - even when people think I shouldn't

Have some secrets - even though some people may think I should tell them or show them everything

Choose to be alone sometimes   - even if everybody else is with someone

Say no sometimes - especially to strangers and bullies

Complain when it's not fair - even though I may still have to do it, or not do it

Be proud when I do well — even though some people may be upset because I did better than them

"Confident Children" by Gael Lindenfield taken from "Becoming Emotionally Intelligent" by Catherine Corrie

Building Self-Esteem

Wanting our children to be happy, loving and successful is natural. A powerful means by which this will be achieved is the way in which they view themselves. The way they view themselves is dependent on the significant people in their lives believing in them and having faith in their potential. A model for building and maintaining self-esteem that we find helpful has been devised by Alistair Smith in his work on accelerated learning. It is known as the BASICS model. Here are 5 tips for each aspect that work well in families.

B is for Belonging

- Including children is an important part of this book and in most chapters there is a section "Child's perspective".

- Take into account a child's view and help to build their sense of self and individuality.

- Create opportunities for all to be included in decision making such as how to spend family time or what meals to eat.

- Encourage children to mix with their peers and with the wider community.

- Develop family traditions and encourage all to take part. See Chapter 9.

- Make good use of photographs and video to capture family history and events.

A is for Aspirations

- Help children to know they can improve.

- Beware of labelling as a shorthand way of commenting on behaviour and tells the child nothing about what could be changed. It could hurt and may be limiting and could even become a self-fulfilling prophecy.

- Children often label themselves, limiting their potential with phrases such as, "I'm the sporty one", "I can't do maths", "I'll never be able to do that" "I don't have any friends". Listen out for these and challenge their perception by questioning and adding the word 'yet' to a statement with 'can't' in it.

- Talk about people they admire and discuss how they overcame obstacles in order to succeed. Are they able to relate this to their own difficulties? Remind them of challenges they have faced and the skills and attributes they used to overcome them?

- Point out to children just how much progress they have already made by looking back at past school books, awards, photographs, achievements in a range of activities sporting or otherwise.

- Build the capacity in children to be able to assess for themselves how well they are doing and what is needed to improve. This is much more powerful and sustainable than only paying attention to what others say.

S is for Safety

- This relates to emotional as well as physical safety, helping children be free from intimidation.

- Make your home a "no put-down zone" where intimidation and ridicule are not allowed, such as, "Leave that alone, you clumsy boy!"

- Avoid talking to others about your children's shortcomings within their hearing, such as, "He is such a nuisance, always interfering."

- Beware of creating guilt such as, "Don't you think your father's got enough to worry about?" Be careful to avoid sarcasm and mixed messages such as, "Off you go with your friends, don't worry about me!"

- Make sure boundaries for behaviour are clear and consistently applied. Distinguish the behaviour from the child whether good or bad.

- Most children are unaware of physical dangers. While we want them to face some challenges, it is our responsibility to keep them safe, whether in the home, on the roads, with strangers, around water, electricity, plants, animals and physical pursuits.

I is for Identity

- Value their unique contributions.

- Love your children uniquely. Each child will have different needs and at different times. It's OK to give time and attention as and when is appropriate rather than trying to be scrupulously fair and even-handed.

- Demonstrate your belief in their ability and potential – say it, don't just think it! Tell them stories about their childhood even if it makes them squirm. Watch out for taking pride in behaviour likely to cause trouble later such as, "She is such a flirt. She'll break a few hearts." Instead praise effort and resilience, which will help develop these attributes.

- Avoid making comparisons with other children such as, "You are just as bad / not as good as your brother / the boy next door."

- Have conversations with your child to understand how they think about themselves and the world and what matters to them. Listen to their answers without judgement and encourage other family members to do the same. Later in this chapter we have some ideas for questions that should be used in a fun way rather than as an interrogation!

- Develop a child's decision-making skills by offering choices, such as which outfit they may wish to wear from your choice of two or three. Similarly, ask for ideas about meal choices for the family.

C is for challenge.

- Encourage and support them as they move out of their comfort zone and try new things.

- Encourage the acquisition of new skills which, dependent upon the age of the child, could be using scissors, riding a bike, learning to swim, playing an instrument, learning a new language or mastering cooking a dish. Being a lifelong learner is one of the greatest attributes we can develop in a child.

- Discuss challenges you have faced and how you overcame them. Let children see how, in your adult life, you use the skills you developed as a child. For example, learning to read means that you can now work in a job you enjoy.

- If a child isn't ready to take on a new challenge yet, consider their concerns. Encourage without pressure and come back to it. They may just be tired and we want them to feel good when they try new things.

- Appreciate the differences between people about what they see as a challenge. One child might regard going to a party with horror and be far outside their comfort zone, bordering on stress. This may not bother another child, even from the same family.

- There is a risk in allowing children to remain in their 'safe' zone as they will feel they have permission to avoid things they find difficult. For example, excusing a child from basic politeness when meeting new people, by saying they are 'shy' does them no favours and may cause difficulties in later life. Give them the push they might need and encourage them to consider how others might be feeling. Let them rehearse the language beforehand to give them confidence.

S is for success.

- Catch them doing well and improving – help them feel the satisfaction of success.

- What do you mean by success? There are many views on this. Our personal view has been captured in this poem, often attributed to Ralph Waldo Emerson, although it may be from a publication by Bessie Stanley in 1905.

Success

To laugh often and much;
to win the respect of intelligent people
  and the affection of children;
to earn the appreciation of honest critics
  and endure the betrayal of false friends;
to appreciate beauty; to find the best in
others;
to leave the world a bit better,
  whether by a healthy child,
  a garden patch
  or a redeemed social condition;
to know even one life has breathed easier
  because you have lived.
This is to have succeeded.

- Ensure all have opportunities to succeed and celebrate when they do. Each time children recognise they have been successful or hear praise, it builds strong positive self-belief, which they can draw upon when facing a challenge. It also means they are more able to be generous in acknowledging others.

- Make praise specific about what they brought to the achievement, not just the achievement itself, so that children understand what it was that made them successful and will be able to apply it to the next situation.

- Teach children to visualise and, therefore, rehearse the 'look' and experience the 'feel' of success before they do something. This helps train the body and mind for the new challenge.

- Beware of giving mixed messages such as saying you only want your child to be happy and then showing your dissatisfaction if they don't achieve academically or sportingly.

Personal Story

When my son was about 8 he was having trouble with an older boy who was threatening him. My first instinct was to go and sort it out with the school, the boy's parents etc. I paused and asked him what he thought would help. He came up with an idea to talk to an older boy in this troublesome boy's class, effectively asking him to keep an eye out for him. This happened and the problem was sorted —my son felt empowered and of course that in itself helps with esteem.

Anonymous

Triggers

Here are 28 triggers to generate conversations for all the family about themselves, likes, dislikes, hopes and fears. There is space for you to add another 2 of your own.

1. *What is your favourite food?*

2. *What food do you dislike most?*

3. *If you were an animal, which one would you be?*

4. *What would you do with a £100 gift?*

5. *Which fictional character would you most like to be?*

6. *If you could choose one super power what would it be and why?*

7. *If you ruled the world, what one thing would you change?*

8. *What do you like most about yourself?*

9. *What embarrasses you?*

10. *What would you like to change about yourself?*

11. *What would you like to change about mum / dad / siblings / teachers / friends?*

12. *What do you want to be when you grow up?*

13. *What do you worry about?*

14. *What frightens you?*

15. *What do you like best about your mum / dad / siblings / friends / teachers?*

16. *Do you have a best friend? Who is your best friend and what is special about them?*

17. *Where would you go to if you had a problem?*

18. *If you had one wish, what would it be and why?*

19. *What would your worst day include?*

20. *Describe your perfect day.*

21. *What makes you angry?*

22. *What makes you laugh?*

23. *Who do you admire?*

24. *Describe a happy memory.*

25. *What is your dream house?*

26. *What do you think has been the greatest invention and why?*

27. *What would you like to invent?*

28. *If you could have your own planet, what would it be like?*

29. _____

30. _____

"Any child can tell you that the sole purpose of a middle name is so he can tell when he's really in trouble."

Dennis Fakes

Communication

Because we may have less time than we would like for our relationships with children, partner, friends, our childcare provider and work colleagues, our communication needs to be as effective as we can make it. The need to have feelings understood is important at any age and is significant in building children's self esteem and emotional intelligence from a very early age. It becomes even more important as they get older.

You will find several references in this book to good communication.

Here are 6 tips

1

Is your child able to talk to you about anything that is going on in their life? You can encourage them if you really listen and avoid leaping in with your own judgements. It must be a two-way thing. It's not just about telling your child something or giving advice but rather listening to their viewpoint and accepting emotions. Allow space for them to respond. Silence can be useful for processing thoughts.

2

Talking is not the only part of the communication process. Listening is an important skill too. Stop what you're doing and give full attention to your child. Make eye contact. Don't interrupt too quickly. Give prompts: nodding, smiling, saying "mmm".

3

Make it clear that you're always willing to give a sympathetic hearing, whether it's about a falling out with a friend, a failure to make the football team or disappointing marks in an exam. Stress that making mistakes is the way to learn how to get things right, not just about failure.

4

Reflective listening is the most effective way of communicating. Recognise, respect and acknowledge your child's views and worries. Look for the emotional meaning that often lies behind the words, identify the feeling and feed it back. Say something such as, "So you must have felt angry when that happened." You can also reflect back the content of what your child is saying to clarify points: "You mean your teacher will be leaving at the end of term?"

5

Communication should be open not closed, unless it is an instruction. For example, "Tell me about how the

school trip went" rather than "Did you enjoy the
school trip?"

6

Setting up good communication when children are
young gives you a head start for the teen years, when
you (both!) might face hormonal changes and the
topics become complicated. As teenagers their skills,
knowledge and experience will have increased and
with a foundation of trust, you can use the pre-teen
years to open up discussions on moral issues and other
topics such as sex, alcohol and drugs.

There are different styles of communication
encompassing a range of additional skills. As parents
we all use most of these styles everyday and they vary
according to the circumstance, age and maturity of the
child. All communication is affected by the timing, the
volume and tone of voice we use as well as our body
language. Being congruent with our feelings and
words, will ensure our messages are more effective.
As you read the following examples bear these points
in mind.

Style	Example	Related Skill
Telling	"Stay away from the fire!"	Being clear and assertive.
Information	"Your teacher said that homework has to be in tomorrow."	Leaving them to respond. Giving information to help them decide what to do.
Advice	"I think it would help to patch up your argument if you invited your friend round to tea."	Offering solutions/ideas.
Sharing	"I had a hard day at work – how was your day?"	Relating and encouraging without judgement.
Negotiating	"I need your bedroom to be tidied so if you do it now we can then play a game together."	Expressing your own needs while accommodating theirs. A win:win solution.
Coaching	"What do you want?" "What's it like?" "What could you do?" "What will you do?"	Encouraging independent thought and decision making.

Style	Example of a 5 year old needing to put on school uniform and leave in the next 10 minutes
Telling	"Put your school uniform on now!"
Information	"Your teacher insists on everyone wearing school uniform and being on time."
Advice	"You will probably get into trouble if you break the school rules."
Sharing	"I can't go to work in my jeans and tee shirt and I wish I could. I have to work with the rules too."
Negotiating	"If you get into your uniform before I count to 100 we will have time to call and pick up your friend on the way to school".

Coaching NB *probably no time for this until after school but worth doing!*	"When you don't want to get ready in time I get worried you will be late and shout at you. You get upset. What can we do? " "Tell me what you were thinking and feeling this morning. We can't change these school rules so how can we do this without being cross with each other? Any other ideas? So, what shall we do?"

Style	Example of a teenager wanting to have alcohol at their own party
Telling	"You can have beer, wine or cider but no spirits."
Information	"Mixing drinks can affect some people strongly making them very ill quickly."
Advice	"It would be a good idea if you got a money contribution from your friends rather than them bringing their own drink."
Sharing	"I can remember a friend of yours being at a party that ended up with someone being very ill and the house got trashed, despite the care taken by the party giver."
Negotiating	"I am happy to buy a crate of beer if you agree to no spirits."
Coaching	"What alcohol did you have in mind?" "What ideas have you heard of to ensure people don't drink too much?" "Which parties have you been to that worked well in managing the drinking?" "What will you do?"

Developing Emotional Intelligence

"If you judge people, you have no time to love them."

Mother Teresa.

Emotional intelligence is a term coined by Daniel Goleman to describe the ways in which we successfully manage our emotions. Building a child's self-esteem is a sound basis for developing emotional intelligence. This in turn enables a child to:

Enhance interpersonal skill.

Increase achievement, optimism and enjoyment.

Reduce feelings of isolation and depression.

Help to connect thinking and feeling.

Develop a range of qualities such as resilience, courage, initiative, tolerance, respect and self-control.

The term emotional intelligence usually includes five aspects:

1 Self-awareness.

This is about knowing yourself and your feelings and using them to make choices and decisions

2 Managing emotions.

The ability to control your feelings

3 Self-motivation.

The ability to persist in the face of setbacks and to motivate yourself

4 Empathy.

Being able to relate to how others are feeling

5 Management of relationships.

The ability to handle feelings in relationships, cooperate in groups and even take the lead.

If we think about these aspects we will probably recognise where our own strengths lie and where we might need to do a little work on ourselves. We can help a child to develop these aspects just as we can help to develop their self-esteem. Here are some ideas.

Self-Awareness - 5 Ideas

1

Encourage them to think about how they learn best. You can do this by getting them to talk about a time when they were successful at learning something and what they did to help themselves.

2

Encourage them to assess themselves rather than relying on feedback from others.

3

Talk about how characters in stories might be feeling and how their situation might make them feel.

4

Ask how a piece of music, art or an event has made them feel.

5

Use a book such as, "Would You Rather?" by John Burningham as a basis for discussion.

Managing Emotions – 5 Ideas

1

Challenge negative or worrying thoughts by pointing out inaccuracies. For example, if they say, "Nobody likes me" , you might reply with, "I thought x was your best friend". Ask how a favourite cartoon character such as Bart Simpson might handle a particular situation to give them an alternative perspective.

2

Teach relaxation techniques to help with times of stress.

3

Use stories to demonstrate how others manage feelings such as the book, "A Huge Bag of Worries" by Virginia Ironside and Frank Rodgers.

4

Collect techniques to use such as 'alphabet spaghetti'. If someone's words are upsetting, imagine they are split into individual letters and float away like alphabet spaghetti. In this way you hear the words but they don't hurt so much.

5

Teach ways to manage anger and calming down before acting in haste. Try the technique, 'wait for the bus'. The child imagines waiting at a bus stop and seeing the bus arrive. The bus takes the problem away and as it moves, the imagined distance provides a sense of perspective about the issue. Alternatively, hitting a pillow can safely release pent-up anger.

Self-Motivation – 5 Ideas

1

Encourage them to talk about things they would like to become, be better at or achieve.

2

Play games such as, "I bet I could". Family members or friends indicate things they might like to try such as, "I bet I could swim four lengths by the end of the month" or "I bet I could learn a new spelling by Friday" or "I bet I could write this report by the end of the week". Record them in some way and check on progress every so often.

3

Ensure praise is specific. The feedback is then useful as information for them to use on the next challenge they come across.

4

Help to go through the steps to success in their head as a kind of rehearsal.

5

Point out any improvements they make in a variety of skills and show them how they relate to any new challenges they are facing. Even if they fail, there will be lots of learning from the experience so look for the skills and knowledge gained.

Empathy – 5 Ideas

1

Develop their listening skills by helping them to reflect not just on the content of what is being said but also on the underlying feelings of a friend, fictional character or family member.

2

Encourage reflection on the impact of actions with questions such as "when that happened, how do you think it made him / her feel?" Help children to notice non-verbal communication such as whether the expression on someone's face and their body language match the words they are using.

3

Develop discussion and debating skills through lots of opportunities with family and friends, encouraging respect for each other's viewpoints.

4

Imaginative play is also a great way for children to discover what it might be like to be someone else.

5

The inevitable conflict between siblings and friends is so useful in examining how individuals might be feeling about something; so don't be afraid of it. Use it in the safe environment of home to explore differences and how to manage them.

Management of Relationships – 5 Ideas

1

Ensure children understand and keep the basic rules about appropriate behaviour in social settings such as listening as well as talking.

2

Develop the notion of rights and responsibilities in a range of situations.

3

Encourage children to take turns in leading groups whether within the family or with friends. It doesn't always have to be the oldest or the loudest who gets to be the leader!

4

Teach cooperation through games that need you all to take turns.

5

Talk through conflict situations with a series of questions based on: What is the situation? What are your options? What are the likely consequences of each option? What is the best solution?

This poem is frequently voted as the UK's favourite in annual surveys. For us, it actually sums up the key aspects of emotional intelligence.

If

By Rudyard Kipling

If you can keep your head when all about you
Are losing theirs and blaming it on you,
If you can trust yourself when all men doubt you,
But make allowance for their doubting too;
If you can wait and not be tired by waiting,
Or being lied about, don't deal in lies,
Or being hated, don't give way to hating,
And yet don't look too good, nor talk too wise:

If you can dream - and not make dreams your master;
If you can think - and not make thoughts your aim;
If you can meet with Triumph and Disaster
And treat those two impostors just the same;
If you can bear to hear the truth you've spoken
Twisted by knaves to make a trap for fools,
Or watch the things you gave your life to, broken,
And stoop and build 'em up with worn-out tools:

If you can make one heap of all your winnings
And risk it on one turn of pitch-and-toss,

And lose, and start again at your beginnings
And never breathe a word about your loss;
If you can force your heart and nerve and sinew ·
To serve your turn long after they are gone,
And so hold on when there is nothing in you
Except the Will which says to them: 'Hold on!'

If you can talk with crowds and keep your virtue,
' Or walk with Kings - nor lose the common touch,
if neither foes nor loving friends can hurt you,
If all men count with you, but none too much;
If you can fill the unforgiving minute
With sixty seconds' worth of distance run,
Yours is the Earth and everything that's in it,
And - which is more - you'll be a Man, my son!

Building Children's Independence

"You know your children are growing up when they stop asking where they came from and refuse to tell you where they're going."

PJ O'Rourke

We are aware that there has been a decline in parents allowing their children the freedom to play outside, explore and develop independence. Rare, yet high profile, cases of child abductions and murders, have made parents increasingly fearful for their children's safety. All parents need to make up their own minds about this issue, thinking about the individual child concerned, the environment and any available support. There is no magical age at which a child might be considered old enough to walk to school alone or be responsible for a younger sibling. It really does depend on the circumstances. One of the biggest steps to children's independence is for them to manage when you're not there and be able to contact someone else if they need to. Most of the working mums in our group have reported the increased rate of their children's language development to be a definite plus side to working. This may simply be because they haven't had mum or dad anticipating their every need and, therefore, have had to ask for what they want from someone else.

As a working parent we may not always be there when our children push boundaries or try new experiences and skills. We, therefore, need to think through our approaches on some of the issues before they occur. Our approach is to focus on building a child's skills so they can ultimately be independent. We will then have done our job as a parent. Remember doing less for your children will help everyone – you will be less worn-out and they will be more skilled. Appreciate them when they do things without being asked or when they make an effort. Affirming children is very powerful.

Here are some useful tips to try at varying stages of a child's development.

Potty training

You cannot potty train an eight month old. If they can't walk or talk they cannot be trained. Regardless of what your parents/in-laws did when their children were small it needs to work for you. These 8 ideas may help

1

Guide them to use the potty or toilet seconds before you think they want to go (watch for signs).

2

When their nappy has been dry for longer periods they may be ready to start to use the loo.

3

Waiting until they can tell you they need to go makes life easier.

4

Dress them in clothes they can easily manage such as pull up trousers. Wendy's family refer to dungarees as "flippin' 'eck trousers" after her father took her two year old son to the gents when on a walk in the park.

It took him a very long time to work out the mechanics of getting these trousers undone and when he emerged, worn out, her son asked why Grandpapa called his outfit "flippin' 'eck trousers"!

5

Have the potty around so they can use it if they wish. If they really don't want to, then leave it.

6

Once started with training try to keep going.

7

Some children respond well to pull-up pants. Others find them indistinguishable from an ordinary nappy, which doesn't help.

8

Summertime or holidays are good times to start the process. You may have more time and playing outside means accidents are no big deal.

10 more steps to personal independence

1

Encourage your child to dress him/herself as soon as possible. They should be pretty competent by the time they start school. Dressing and undressing can take most of a PE lesson at school, leaving little time for exercise. On non-school days, Wendy gave her children a choice of two outfits to wear so they learnt about choices, but didn't spend hours going through all their clothes.

2

Teach them to tell the time as soon as they are able. Penny and her husband taught their boys the time they considered it was OK to get up in the morning and they were expected to stay in bed until that time. At a later stage, the older one learned how to make tea and to bring it up to them. The younger one trailed behind with the biscuit tin. It didn't last that long but was glorious while it did!

3

Teach your child to cook. It encourages even the youngest child to eat and the older ones to take their share in preparing family meals. They can also bake those cakes for the school fair, and save you a job. Make preparing family meals a joint exercise. Even the smallest child can do simple tasks like arranging food on a plate. Having two sons, Penny was anxious they would never be dependent on a female for their food. Both sons cook well and one is even passionate about the art. By contrast, some of their girlfriends have not been that interested.

4

Teach your child about keeping safe at home. According to ROSPA/NSPCC most children under 13 are not mature enough to cope with an emergency and should not be left alone for more than a short time. Talk through a variety of scenarios to help them prepare. Do they know how to contact the emergency services? Do they have any basic first aid? What about answering the door and the telephone? Could they get out of the house in the dark or in a hurry?

5

Teach your child about keeping safe outside the home. Walking without an adult to a neighbour's, a friend's or to school, going to the post-box or to a local shop can all seem huge milestones. Consider trialling some of these activities while you are on holiday when you have more time to teach safety and can practise together. What about keeping safe while travelling? The advice by ROSPA and NSPCC at the time of writing this book, is that children should be over 7 years before being allowed to cross the road alone. Under this age they cannot judge distances and speed correctly enough. Teach them strategies for if they are ever uneasy about the behaviour of a stranger in a public place. Encourage them to draw the attention of others to the situation and not to fear any personal embarrassment this might cause.

6

Teach your child about money. Encourage them to save for something through pocket money, gifts or earnings (within the child labour laws of course!). Going to a nearby shop to buy something is good practice for knowing what things cost and checking change. Help them to be aware of being safe with money and keeping it securely hidden.

7

Encourage independent play. This has the added bonus of giving you a little time for yourself.

8

Encourage personal responsibility. Learning to be responsible for their own entertainment, organisation and motivation will be helpful once they start school and have to remember things such as homework, games kit and revision. Show them how to plan ahead and share some of your own planning methods with them.

9

Teach your child to be responsible for others. At the time of writing this book advice from NSPCC and ROSPA is that anyone under 16 cannot be held responsible for children in their care and that under 16's should not be left alone over night. Views about this often differ. Check the latest advice from your local county council. Whatever you decide, think about the child's level of maturity and comfort. Once Penny's older son was mature enough to 'baby sit' his younger brother, she and her husband insisted the boys stayed up. They often had a video and snacks to make it more fun. In this way, if there was an emergency to be handled they would be awake and, therefore, better equipped to make good judgements.

10

Encourage your child to understand that with extra freedom there will be extra responsibilities.

Here are 4 areas for consideration.

1

Whatever your views of mobile phones, they can be very useful tools for parents wanting to keep in touch with their children. They also provide a good opportunity for teaching levels of independence about issues such as budgeting for their phone and taking care of costly possessions. You may wish to have rules about how they use them and do check what the policy is at your child's school. A cautionary note - mobile phones can hinder independence if they are used to call home about a problem which they could probably solve themselves.

2

You may have a wide choice of out of school activities in your area, which you would like your child to try.

Having made a choice, take the opportunity to develop a sense of responsibility. Discuss the kind of commitment the activity may involve, such as financial, practice, giving notice and turning up regularly.

3

Establish some rules about internet usage for your children, whether they are at home or at friends. Make them aware of the dangers of chat rooms. There are some good websites that provide helpful tips on how to protect your children.

4

All the following push the boundaries towards greater independence and provide opportunities to discuss keeping safe, taking responsibility, caring for others and property and complying with legal obligations:

Choices about drink, drugs, smoking, circles of friends

First pop gig/festival

First party at your house both when you're in or out

First holiday with friends

Learning to drive

Going out with friends who are driving

Girlfriend/boyfriend staying the night

Sex

Talk about these issues before they happen as it can reduce tension and heated emotion. You will then have a foundation on which to build the conversation when needed.

Here are 3 thoughts about finance

1

Having their own money will encourage independence and taking responsibility. This may come from earning pocket money by taking on jobs around the house or part-time employment. Or you may choose to provide an allowance from which they will need to pay for agreed items.

2

Wendy had an agreement with her children that she would provide the money for a basic version of an item, such as trainers. However if they wanted brand-named shoes then they made up the difference from their own money.

3

Holidays are another opportunity to help children be aware of costs and budgeting. They might have a special holiday allowance from which they buy sundry items.

Teenagers

"The average income of the modern teenager is about 2 a.m."

http://www.quotegarden.com/teenagers.html

We attended a great parenting course, Parentlink, led by the wonderful facilitator, Margaret Wainwright. One of our follow up sessions covered some of the difficulties we face in bringing up teenagers. A book on this topic that we found helpful is "Get out of my life but first take me and Alex into town" by Tony Wolf and Suzanne Franks. Here are some notes we took from the session:

1

Only give advice to teenagers if they want it. They are more likely to listen.

2

Remember to take care of yourself as you will then be more able to take care of others.

3

Don't handle all their issues. Encourage them to take responsibility for themselves.

4

Be clear and specific when making requests. Decide what is non-negotiable and be consistent. Pick your battles so you don't end up fighting about every small thing.

5

Don't be surprised if they say hurtful things which seem out of character. As they struggle for independence they are likely to try to test you in the safety of your relationship. Stay calm and carry on! When the heat of the emotion has passed try and find out what the underlying issues are and understand their feelings. One tip we learnt was that, although teenagers are neither adults nor children, it sometimes helps to take 10 years off their age to understand the toddler-type behaviour you are dealing with.

6

Show respect for yourself. Remember you are a very important role model. Don't allow yourself to be taken for granted.

7

If you are doing something for them and they show no appreciation or civility, you might like to ask yourself and them "Why am I doing this. What's in it for me?" If there is no satisfactory response, you may choose to stop doing it.

8

Don't "overfeed" them by anticipating and fulfilling their every need. They will need to understand and learn to meet their own needs and wants.

9

You may find that teenage boys feel the need to take more risks, often physical. It is hard for us as our instincts are to protect them and finding the balance is a struggle between encouraging them to challenge themselves and keeping safe.

10

Without being over protective, be aware of what is going on in your teenagers life, such as the friends they have, what is in their bedrooms and changes in their behaviour, so that you are informed.

11

Expect good behaviour and praise and acknowledge it.

12

If you are a single parent, look for support from others during what can be a testing time.

8 pointers from a step-parent we talked to on supporting step-children as well as your 'own'

1. Let birth parent take time out with children individually. Take a back seat. Don't try to replace their parent.

2. Let them think about their relationship with you. If they feel no pressure, they have the space to come to you if they wish. Remember your relationship is very different from the one they have with their real parent.

3. *Express your own values but don't take the lead on discipline. Don't hold grudges. Keep communication open.*

4. *Enable bonding between step-children and new babies by encouraging involvement at all levels.*

5. *Being non-judgemental means they can build their relationship with you.*

6. *Be aware that the step-parent label can be a negative one. Chances are conflict would arise in any family not just where there are step-parents.*

7. *Stand in their shoes. Look to understand their point of view.*

8. *Have a long-term view about developing your relationship.*

Chapter Eight

Being Involved in Your Child's Education

"One thing about parents is that no matter what stage your child is in, the parents who have older children always tell you the next stage is worse."

Dave Barry

Whether you are in paid work or not, there is no doubt that you are involved in your child's education from the moment they are born. You don't have to be at the school gate each day or be available to help out in the classroom to be involved so don't underestimate your influence and, whatever you do, don't feel guilty about not being available during school hours. Did you know that on average, children are in school for less than 15% of their waking hours? This means there is a huge amount of time when other people impact on their learning and development. In spite of this we all worry about choosing schools, getting them ready for this big transition in their lives and continuing to support them whatever their age. The tips and pointers in this chapter will help you do the best you can.

Choosing pre-school education – 12 tips

1

Your choices for pre-school children are for them: to remain at home with your childcare provider or to attend the local playgroup; a state nursery; workplace nursery; private nursery or a specialist nursery such as Montessori. Your choice will depend on: the location and ease of access for you or your carer; your financial situation; the friendships being built with other families in the area; your child's development and current needs.

2

It is important to know how accommodating your pre-school provider can be. You may need to discuss whether there is any flexibility in the hours your child can attend to suit you, your child, your family and the demands of your work.

3

Some pre-schools have associated mother and toddler groups and are a useful way of getting to understand their approach and values. Even if you can't attend, encourage your childcare provider to go along as they may give you further information to help with your choice. It may also help them to build friendships for your child as well as for themselves.

4

Many primary schools have nurseries attached. Don't assume that your child will automatically be given a place at the primary school. The primary school operates as a separate entity with different entry criteria. Do check out the situation by asking for the admissions criteria. Typically, local authorities make decisions about school placements based on where the child lives, but this isn't the case for nurseries. This means that priority must be given to children living in specific roads, commonly known as the catchment area. If you don't live in this specified area, your child may not get a place, even if they were at the nursery. Sometimes the number of placements at the nursery doesn't even match the admission number for the main school.

5

Children make huge developmental strides in their first five years and any pre-school provision should be meeting a range of needs. Typically such provision should cater for a child's physical, social and emotional development through a wide variety of activities.

6

Get a feel for the attitudes the providers have towards children and parents, the importance of play and local schools. Structured play is crucial to a child's development so it is wise to find a provider that makes this aspect its key focus.

7

Children learn best through play so check there is a wide variety of experiences on offer to develop large and fine motor skills as well as language, creativity, imagination and socialisation. With this grounding, the more formal requirements of education such as reading and writing skills, will come later. Indeed, children with a solid foundation of play-based activities tend to read and write much more quickly.

8

Take a good look around at the building, facilities and equipment so that you can assess the care and thinking that has shaped the provision. Use the check list in this chapter.

9

Consider the aims of the organisation. For whom does it exist?

10

Note the way in which the place is organised. Are you happy with aspects of safety, the structure of the sessions on offer and the range of activities for children? Do they have access to the outdoor environment?

11

If you witness children misbehaving, are you happy with the approaches used by the staff? Children need to be taught how to behave and not shouted at, or worse. Ask about the punishment/reward system in operation to help you decide whether you are comfortable with their approach.

12

If you are in employment, your company may subscribe to the childcare voucher scheme which can provide some financial benefits. The rules on these change from time to time so check out the latest information - www.hmrc.gov.uk/childcare and follow the links to childcare vouchers.

6 things to consider when choosing a school

1

Do make time for a visit and, if possible, when the school is in session to give you a greater understanding.

2

People often talk about a 'gut' reaction when visiting and choosing a school. As a parent you sense whether an environment will be right for your child. While this is a good piece of advice, for those who wish for a more structured approach the checklist which follows for evaluating a school is helpful. The checklist is divided into three key areas: the building; the attitudes and philosophy: and in the classroom.

3

Do talk to others with experience of the schools you have in mind. There are bound to be conflicting views. Consider whose opinion you value most when listening to the comments of others.

4

OFSTED is the government body that inspects schools on a regular basis. Their reports, which cover a range of aspects of teaching and learning, are publicly available on the internet.

5

At the time of print, annual league tables of national tests are available. It is helpful to remember that these reflect only some aspects of school life and only those areas that are measurable.

6

When you are thinking about school choices, the start time in the day is very important - could you drop them off occasionally? Does the school offer extended hours provision such as breakfast and after school clubs?

A handy checklist for the evaluation of a primary school

The building:

The Playground.

1. Is it clean, tidy and safe?

2. What is the condition of the fixed playground apparatus?

3. Is there a field, garden or other location for an outdoor classroom?

4. Are there litter baskets and are they in good repair?

The Entrance.

1. Is it attractive?

2. Is it welcoming?

3. Is there a suitable waiting area?

4. Do you have an impression of what's important to the school by looking at the displays and by the way in which you are treated on arrival?

The Classrooms

1. Is your first impression one of a stimulating child-centred environment?

2. Is there adequate heating, lighting, ventilation and access to drinking water?

3. Is there sufficient furniture and is it in a good enough condition?

4. Is there sufficient equipment and is it in good condition?

The Library

1. Is there one?

2. Is it inviting?

3. Are there plenty of books arranged in a well-ordered way?

4. Do the children seem trained in its usage?

The Toilets and Washrooms

1. Are they clean, hygienic and reasonably sweet-smelling?

2. Are they easily accessible?

3. Are there enough?

4. Are they age-appropriate?

The Head's Room

1. Is it welcoming?

2. Are there easy chairs?

3. Is it tidy?

4. Is it both a place for strategic planning and for children?

Attitudes and philosophy: 14 aspects to consider

1 Did you feel welcome? Were you shown courtesy and interest by all you met?

2 How would you describe the attitude of staff towards parents?

3 How did the children react towards visitors?

4 How was authority exercised and received?

5 How did children treat each other?

6 What did you notice about movement around the school?

7 What did you notice about general classroom behaviour?

8 How was poor behaviour managed? Would you be happy for your child to be treated in this way?

9 What out of school activities are provided and for how many children?

10 What links are there between the school and the community?

11 How do children regard the school? Ask!

12 *How do parents regard the school? Ask!*

13 *How do staff regard the school? Ask!*

14 *What kind of parental involvement is encouraged? Is there a "parents' association" or "friends of the school"?*

In the classroom: 10 more considerations

1 *Is there a pleasant, working atmosphere?*

2 *Are the children relaxed, yet purposeful?*

3 *Is the teacher at ease?*

4 *Is there a lively, stimulating and happy learning environment?*

5 *Is there ordered freedom?*

6 *Is the teacher able to get the attention of the whole class?*

7 *Are the children enthusiastic?*

8 *How would you describe the relationship between teacher and children?*

9 *What is the general organisation like?*

10 *Does it feel like a safe environment, physically and emotionally?*

Preparation for school

Your local authority will have a policy about whether children start school at the beginning of the term in which they will be five, commonly known as staggered entry, or whether all children start together in September. This information will be made clear in the school prospectus. During those first few weeks at school, your child may not be expected to attend full time. It may be mornings only or some other reduced week option. This may impact on your childcare arrangements. Children find those first few weeks very tiring so don't try to persuade the staff at school to make an exception by letting your child stay all day.

Once you have a place at a school there are lots of ways you can help your child to prepare for a change, which has been described as the second biggest shock in a child's life. The first one? Being born!

10 ways to prepare your child physically

1

It is important your child can: dress him/herself adequately; feed him/herself adequately; go to the toilet by him/herself and wash hands properly; be equipped with the correct clothing and games kit. Check if children will wear plimsolls during the day before you spend a lot of money on school shoes that they may only wear for a short amount of time.

2

If you have a choice, choose clothes and footwear that will be comfortable for sitting on the floor, jumping, running, walking, bouncing, stretching, bending and sitting on a chair.

3

Children learn best when they are exploring and experimenting so choose clothes that its OK to be messy in and that will wash easily

4

Choose clothes, jackets, shoes and boots that are easy to put on, take off and fasten. Slip-on or Velcro fastened shoes will mean they won't have to worry about tying laces. When teaching children to tie laces, let them sit on your legs and tie your shoelaces. Let them practice taking off a sweater or jacket and putting it back on even if it's inside out. Help your child do up buttons by advising them to start from the bottom and work up.

5

Children should be encouraged to tidy up toys when they have finished playing with them

6

Practice good sitting and listening skills. Have some fun by timing them at home to see how long they can sit for. Use an egg timer for practice.

7

Do ensure the school knows about any medical conditions, special diets, contact details and changes of address.

8

Eating breakfast before school is essential to help your child cope with the demands of the day and helps to establish a healthy habit.

9

Encouraging children to drink water prevents them from becoming de-hydrated which can affect performance.

10

Develop you child's road safety awareness skills in preparation for the journeys to and from school and for any outings that might be organised by the staff.

10 ideas for helping your child psychologically

1

What idea does your child have of school? Write down their responses to this question. Maybe your child could draw a picture of what he or she thinks it will be like.

2

In these early stages, give yourself and your child enough time in the morning for a calm start to the day.

3

Sleep is essential for all.

4

It will ease anxiety if you remember everything your child needs to take each day – a list by the front door may help, or putting everything ready there the night before.

5

Try bringing the school into the home in some way such as inviting children round who are to be in the same class, finding out about what they are learning and talking about the topics at home. Relate things that they will cover at school to your working life, such as writing and listening skills.

6

Prepare your child for routines such as bells, taking turns, queuing. Explain that you also have routines at work.

7

Be positive about school, the staff and learning.

8

Be aware of your own reactions to school and teachers and try to prevent any negative emotions being passed on. Feelings expressed such as, "I hated school" or "I was never any good at maths" can have a huge impact on how your child views school and learning.

9

Schools are much more open, friendlier places these days so don't ever feel afraid of the staff or of the governing body.

10

If you know of any other children starting at the same school, help build new friendships by inviting one or two round to play. Children settle much more quickly if they see a familiar and friendly face in their classroom and in the playground.

10 ideas for supporting your child intellectually

1

Your child has learned a huge amount already and you have been the teacher. This doesn't stop once he or she goes to school. You will simply be sharing the role with others.

2

Your child should be able to say his or her first and last name, names of parents, your telephone number and address.

3

Encourage lots of conversation, a questioning approach and longer concentration spans.

4

Help your child see it is OK to ask questions and give them useful phrases to say if they are unsure such as, "I'm sorry, I don't understand what to do."

5

Listening is a complex skill. Teach good listening skills such as: looking at the person who is speaking; keeping still while you listen; hearing what is said and thinking quietly about it.

6

Encourage them to practise listening quietly when someone is reading a story or a poem.

7

Promote the love of books through reading stories and modelling good practice by reading for pleasure and for reference yourself. Boys benefit from seeing male role models read.

8

If you want to start your child writing at home it will be helpful to find out from the school what writing approach and style they use.

9

Talk about the skills you use in your work and relate them to what they will be learning at school.

10

Praise your child for the effort they make without adding a judgement as to how good you think the work is. This helps the child to assess their own work and encourages them to develop resilience.

4 things to consider during those first few months

1

Don't be surprised if your child is physically and emotionally very tired. It is a big step they have taken. Give them space and relaxation when they come home and accept the signs of an over-tired child.

2

It is quite common for a child to regress once they've started school, especially if there is a younger sibling still at home. They may want feeding, use a bottle or just act like a baby. They soon grow out of this and may just need a little reassurance.

3

The pang of separation may well be strong for both you and your child so be aware. Penny's second son made straight for the young teacher's lap on his first morning of school. Penny had to drive to the school where she was the Head Teacher in tears and go straight to the hall to deliver a meeting to new parents. We guess those parents knew she understood how they were feeling!

4

The first year at school is probably the year when children develop the most. This speed of development is very rewarding for teachers but can be quite surprising for parents.

10 tips for staying involved

1

Your attitude to learning is very important for your child's education. Are you a learner? How do you demonstrate it? Do you and your partner read to your children and read for yourselves, whether for pleasure or work? Children watch adults all the time and model their behaviour. It is instinctive for survival.

2

If you comment on their work do stay positive and be specific. Negative feedback can damage self-esteem and hinder a willingness to learn.

3

Regard the time you have together as quality time and be focused. If you are busily preparing a meal, suggest a time later on when you can have a chat or look at any homework together. This is much better than trying to do both at the same time.

4

Bombarding children with questions about their day never seems to work. They are often happier to talk much later on, maybe over a meal or in the bath. Actually we're all pretty much the same and often prefer to process our day before we talk about it. For a quick assessment a friend of ours would ask her children how their day was, on a scale of 1 – 10. She would give her day a score as well and they would return to the topic much later in the evening if they wished. Talking about your day first may encourage them to share.

5

Provide a home environment in which there are opportunities to continue learning. Allowing children to discover things for themselves will enhance learning. However, some direct teaching is necessary with specific skills such as how to tie shoelaces.

6

Try to avoid giving your children instant solutions to difficulties that arise. Encourage them to work it out for themselves.

7

Volunteer to help out at the school whenever you have the time. There may be a parent- teacher organisation or a vacancy for a form representative role or a position on the governing body. Perhaps you could help out with a trip if you have the flexibility at work. Maybe you have a spare couple of hours during the school day in which you could help hear children read or support in some other way. Perhaps you could take a day off and help on a school trip, or even organise a one-off event for the school such as a fashion evening or a parent-teacher supper.

8

If you want to, and are able, negotiate with your employer, permission to attend anything in which your child is taking part, such as a class assembly or a production like the Christmas play. These are special times, which cannot come back. However be careful about promising your child you will attend sports day as this is weather dependent and you may not be able to go on the rearranged date.

9

If your child is having difficulties with learning, do talk to teachers about it. It may be that the way your child processes new learning has not been fully recognised and/or catered for. Good practice in schools is where the teacher presents new information to be learned in a variety of ways, thereby accommodating a range of learning styles.

10

Talk to a parent who is more involved with the school, and who you trust to help feel connected. This is useful for gathering information and also dispelling rumours that can be widespread and are not always true.

Some useful questions to ask your child about their school day

What was hard for you today?

Did you ask any good questions?

Did you tackle something new?

What did you manage to improve?

Did you make any interesting mistakes?

Did you learn anything useful by watching someone else?

How could you have helped your teacher get that tricky stuff across better?

Are there any ways you would have organised any of the lessons differently?

From Guy Claxton's work on 'Building Learning Power'.

Five Rs for helping children to become good learners.

In his work on accelerated learning, Alistair Smith has devised a model for those helping children become good learners. He calls it the '5Rs' and references the work of Guy Claxton in the book, 'Wise Up'. The 'Rs' in question are: resilience; responsibility, resourcefulness; reasoning; reflection.

1. Resilience

Can we help children 'stick at it' when things get difficult? Yes, by encouraging them to think about how to improve their performance and giving specific praise that demonstrates how they improved.

2. Responsibility

Can we help children look after themselves and others based on moral choices? Yes, by encouraging their questioning and listening skills and praising them when they demonstrate tolerance and consideration for others.

3. Resourcefulness

Can we help children know what to do and where to go if they get stuck? Yes, by helping children to develop a capacity for knowing what to do next, especially if they seem to have reached a dead end. Encouraging good questioning skills will help as well as offering specific praise for when they have shown resourcefulness.

4. Reasoning

Can we help children make careful decisions? Yes, by showing them how to collect evidence, break down a problem and consider it from different angles.

5. Reflection

Can we help children learn from experience and see a range of perspectives? Yes, by spending time understanding what and how learning has taken place. Being able to articulate learning helps to consolidate that learning and enable the learner to make connections and develop.

'The Alps Resource Book' by Alistair Smith and Nicola Call.

Spinning yarns

PUPIL: Teacher, would you punish me for something I didn't do?
TEACHER: Of course not.
PUPIL: Good, because I didn't do my homework.

www.teacherhumor.com

Homework or home learning – 13 things to consider.

1

Schools often use the term 'home learning' rather than 'homework' in order to signify that learning can take many forms, such as having a conversation with a grandparent about differing childhood experiences or collecting artefacts to assist with a project. It is also used to promote reflection on learning and to move away from the negative implications the word 'work' can sometimes have. To engender a love of learning our approach at home should foster the spirit of shared experiences and reflecting on them. This is a long way from ordering our children into a different room and demanding they 'get on with their homework'. Don't, however do it for them!

2

Homework may take the form of simply consolidating what has been taught in class that day, in which case children may be required to do a few sums, write some sentences or complete an assignment.

3

Our brains process in ways unique to each individual which means that your child might learn in a different way from you or from other family members. When supporting their home learning it is useful to tap into your child's particular learning style which may be predominantly visual, auditory, kinaesthetic or a combination of two or all three. In this way, acquisition of new skills and concepts can be most effective. Teachers these days try to present new material in a range of ways so that all pupils can access it in a way that is comfortable for them. Traditional, more formal schooling favours children who are predominantly auditory learners as they tend to process through the written and spoken word. Kinaesthetic learners do best when they can tackle new material in a more practical way, are able to move about, touch and feel things. Visual learners rely heavily on visual cues such as display around the walls, pictures, graphs, photographs and film. Many of us use all these processes but will have varying degrees of preference and blend. If you can tell what works for your child, do deploy their preferred style when they are struggling with new concepts or revising for tests and exams. For more information and questionnaires on learning styles take a look at "The Alps Approach" by Alistair Smith and Nicola Call.

4

Similarly we all have preferences for the way in which we work best and children are no different. Some prefer absolute quiet but others really do work better if there is some background noise. Some prefer a table or desk while others can work well lying on the floor. Some are best if they do their assignments as soon as they get in from school whereas others need to eat, to relax and maybe to exercise before they can settle. Help your child to discover their preferred way of working by trying different things and help them to do what's right for them. However, children need to fit in with family meal times too!

5

It is helpful if you and your child understand the purpose behind any homework given. Some teachers will include information such as whether the homework is about skills practice, research, consolidation, creativity or independent learning. They may also indicate how long an assignment should take and what, if any, should be a parent's input. If this information is not forthcoming, encourage your child to find out.

6

When your child starts school, one of the documents you are likely to receive will be the homework policy outlining the amount of homework and the expectations on children to consolidate their learning at home.

7

Many primary schools have reading diaries so that you can record pages read with you at home. Most secondary schools and some primaries issue each child with a homework diary as a method of communication between teacher and parent. This is the vehicle for informing your child's teacher about any areas of difficulty your child is encountering or explanations about incomplete assignments. Encourage your child to get into the habit of taking these diaries to and from school.

8

Our aim is to engender a love of learning that will be life-long. Learning should be fun; indeed learning is more effective when it is fun. We tend to remember things that have made us laugh or were a little bit quirky. Fun ideas include: having a very personal home-made dictionary in which words are recorded alongside a picture drawn by the child; having key words for learning written on large pieces of paper cut out to resemble stepping stones – the child can jump on each 'stone' as they are able to read the word and travel across the room in this way.

9

Most of us learn best by talking things through. In fact many teachers have introduced the idea of 'talking partners' in their classes so that pupils can rehearse their ideas, express their thoughts and test each other on their learning with a friend. This helps secure the learning as well as clarify thinking prior to the completion of a task. We can harness this good practice at home by inviting a friend round to be a 'homework buddy'. Since we learn best when explaining the learning to someone else, should a friend get stuck, both parties benefit when one teaches the other.

10

An early activity when children start secondary school is to prepare a piece of work which is about them such as their family and friends, likes and dislikes, hobbies, sporting teams they support, books and films enjoyed. If you rehearse with them their thoughts on some of these areas you can help your child to complete this type of assignment and have things to discuss with new friends.

11

If you have a child carer you may wish or need them to help with your child's homework. Talk this through with them so they know what is expected and how you want it handled.

12

As part of a programme of extending schools, some schools now provide homework clubs at the end of the school day. If this might be helpful to your child, consider whether there is a cost involved or whether attendance is dependant on the presence of a parent or carer, as this will have implications for your childcare provision.

13

Many older children will be able to study at home during exam time, commonly known as "study leave". This can cause a problem for working parents if your child can't get to school independently when they need to go into school and if you have no child care provider or one who can drive. It is helpful if you have the exam timetable (for lots of reasons!) and can perhaps share lifts with other parents. If that doesn't work, finding a reliable taxi firm is an option. Some schools may be comfortable with children going into school to study, even when not required to do so.

Spinning Yarn

TEACHER: Did you do your homework?
PUPIL: No, teacher.
TEACHER: Do you have an excuse?
PUPIL: Yes, it's all my mother's fault.
TEACHER: She kept you from doing it?
PUPIL: No, she didn't nag me enough!

www.teacherhumor.com

Parent / Teacher Consultations

Schools hold regular opportunities for parents and teachers to meet to discuss pupil progress. Here are 10 tips for making the best of them.

1

Parent – teacher consultation meetings are typically held in the evenings but sometimes teachers can be released during the school day to meet with parents. The fact that you are unavailable at certain times of the day or evening should not preclude you from having the opportunity to discuss your child's progress.

2

The meeting will be pretty brief, often only about ten minutes, therefore it is helpful to be prepared. Talk with your child beforehand and jot down any questions you both might have or information you need to pass on.

3

If at all possible take your child with you. Penny's son once asked her not to go to the consultation evening during his time in the sixth form as he felt it unfair to talk about him when he wasn't there and the school did not wish students to be present. He explained he would not have a similar conversation with her boss!

Realising the truth in this, she and her husband agreed not to attend. The conversation is about the child's progress and if they can be present it can help foster a responsibility for their own learning. As a kindergarten teacher in America, Penny's cousin, Jennifer, operated a system whereby her pupils aged five and six, were expected to attend consultation meetings, showing their parents the progress they had made and exploring their next steps. In this way, all parties were clear about the feedback given.

4

If it is the school's policy not to have the children present, think carefully about how and when you give your child feedback on what the teacher has said. Make both praise and areas for development specific and focus your language on behaviour and not about the child.

5

In discussion with your child's teacher ask for examples of evidence of anything said about their progress, attitudes to learning, behaviour and social development to avoid misunderstandings. Similarly be prepared to offer examples yourself about your child outside school. In this way, teachers can build a more accurate picture of your child.

6

Listen carefully to the comments made and if it helps, jot things down, reading your notes out loud to the teacher, to establish accuracy.

7

Towards the end of the meeting some targets may be set for your child. Check you understand these, ask how the targets will be measured and explore whether they are achievable given the timescale.

8

Sometimes examples of your child's work will be available for you to look at. Don't be surprised if not every piece of work appears to have been marked. Assessment of children's work may have been done verbally or collectively with others in the class. Any marks on a child's work should indicate how well they achieved the intended outcomes of the piece of work and what they might do to improve next time. A simple tick or a cross doesn't always do this job. If a level has been assigned to a piece of work, don't be afraid to ask how the level has been arrived at and what needs to be done for the next level to be achieved. If in doubt, do ask if you can see the school's marking or assessment policy.

9

So much will have changed since you were at school. So, given there is no such thing as a stupid question, go ahead and ask!

10

Remember the common ground between you and the teacher is that you both want your child to make progress, which means these meetings are very important to you all!

Schools and finance -3 areas for consideration

1

State schools very often need additional funds from parents/parents associations to supplement trips and visiting performers. Contributions are normally voluntary. In most cases it is not legal to charge – though without contributions many of these valuable events wouldn't happen. However, if this is difficult for you then don't hesitate to speak to the staff at the school. A free school lunch system operates in the UK and many other countries, so do investigate if you think your financial situation may warrant this help. Most schools will handle this sensitively so no one would know your child is a recipient.

2

If you feel your child needs extra academic support and your school is unable to provide this, or you haven't the time to investigate what options you have within school, then you might consider private tuition. This can be a couple of sessions before an exam or longer term support for a particular subject. Ask other parents, advertise in local shops or ask at school for recommendations. You may be able to share private tuition with another child to help with the cost.

3

If you are considering private education include in your calculations the annual fees as well as a more costly uniform, trips, increase in child care costs due to longer school holidays, transport costs, music lessons and all extracurricular activities. You may find private schools have the advantages for working parents of a longer school day, homework clubs after school and breakfast clubs for an early drop off. As they operate much more as a business there is generally more of a customer focused approach. Smaller classes are normally a guarantee with private schools but there is no guarantee of a better quality of teaching.

3 miscellaneous tips

1

If for any reason you or the person looking after your child can't pick up him or her up from school and you need to ask someone else to do so, then call the school to let them know. Keep your child safe by explaining what the arrangements are for collecting after school or an activity and talk them through different scenarios and what action they might take. Remind your child not to go home with anyone else. In unusual circumstances, if you had to ask someone to collect your child, who they were not expecting, have a pre-arranged code that they can use, such as the name of their favourite toy.

2

Good communication with your childcare provider continues to be very important and takes on a new dimension when your child attends school. They may have more contact with the staff, other parents and children and you will need to look to them to build and maintain the links that affect your child.

3

Talk about handling some of the pitfalls of being at the school gates as misinformation and rumours can flourish here. It can however, be a great way to find out something of what is going on and for your child to be included in the school community.

Personal Story

We asked a single parent about sharing involvement in her children's education with their father. These are her responses.

What has proved most difficult?

Attending school events, as their father and normally his new partner were there. Selecting schools would have been difficult, but the primary school was chosen before the divorce and there was little or no choice at secondary.

What solutions have you found?

Trying to work out who else might be at events on their own as well and making a beeline for them on arrival or asking them to save me a seat etc. Telling children that I would be there, but not to expect me to find them afterwards if Dad was around & they were going home with him; we could speak later.

Has anything surprised you?

That school contact lists (snow charts/ PTA ones etc) often make no allowance for separated parents and therefore messages do not always get through. Teachers do not pass on info. from one year to the next that children's parents are separated. Take an early opportunity to advise form teacher and ask them to let colleagues know as situation can cause problems (see below).

Has homework been an issue? If so, in what ways and what tips do you have?

Books (& equipment & kit) can be in the wrong house for homework (or school the next day). Use a USB stick for homework on the computer or get them to email themselves. Forward planning is a skill the children have to learn for themselves quickly. It does go wrong though and discrete letters/emails to school can help avoid criticism, but they are not always very understanding of a child who leaves homework to the last minute and then doesn't have the books. Homework can be done on a separate sheet and pasted in another day sometimes.

What about parent/teacher consultations?

Schools seem prepared (in theory) to offer separate appointments to each parent (I couldn't cope with going as a threesome with the new wife). However quite often they don't have enough slots to see each child's parents as a couple let alone separately. Also as nowadays most children have to book appointments with teachers, it is too embarrassing for them to explain why they need two sets of appointments and no one has ever taken this responsibility on for them (even at primary school). Teachers are sometimes prepared to chat on the phone to you instead at another time, if you explain the circumstances. Hopefully things might be better for you.

How have the schools handled your situation?

See above. Generally poorly, although they do seem to be able to keep admin records that prompt the sending of copies of reports to each parent. I would have liked the school to have agreed a protocol about "signing up" for school trips. There were several occasions of the ex getting the invite slip via the child; replying positively and the school then insisting I pay when he defaulted!

What have been the advantages and disadvantages for the children?

Advantages: forward planning, Disadvantages: different take on school feedback. Additional sets of uniform required otherwise washing etc a challenge

Is there anything you would have done differently? Would this be the same for all your children?

Ensure you tell other parents/ teachers about your circumstances as early as possible (send a letter into class day one) so your children don't get into difficult positions. So often it is still assumed that children have one father and one mother. (Make a card for mother on Mother's day (& my step mum?) draw your family tree (how do I show my half brothers & sisters), get your mother to make a cake (but I am at Dad's this weekend; will the step mum do?) As I got used to the situation I found ways of letting the parents of new classmates know about the domestics ASAP. ("I'll just check whether S is with me that w/e or at her father's" even when you know she is with you; preferably within earshot of a number of other mums, the gossip will spread very quickly!) Otherwise parents can arrive to collect from wrong house, ring wrong number, call you by the step mum's name as they have clocked her name, assume she is the mother & you are the hired help etc. Children themselves do not like to offer up explanation of their domestics and this can lead to difficult social situations for them.

Have there been any differences between primary and secondary schools on these issues?

By secondary school they are not normally the only child with divorced parents. They are not required to involve their parents in things so much, as they take on more personal responsibility. There are fewer events that you are asked to attend so not so much opportunity for having to get around the sports day events/ find a seat at the school production without bumping into the ex & his family etc. Children also largely making their own decisions about subjects to study, extra curricular activities etc.

A child returned from his first day at school looking rather fed up. His mother asked him what was the matter. He replied he was fed up because he hadn't had a present. Probing a little further, she asked what he meant by that. He replied his teacher had asked him "to sit there for the present."

Adapted from "Cider with Rosie" by Laurie Lee.

Chapter Nine

Making the Most of Family Traditions and Holidays

"Family values are a little like family vacations - subject to changeable weather and remembered more fondly with the passage of time. Though it rained all week at the beach, it's often the momentary rainbows that we remember."

Leslie Dreyfous

You might have guessed by now that we are passionate about doing our best for children and giving them all we can to help in their all-round development. To our relief we have discovered that being part of a family does this job well, whether the parents work or not. Phew!! In this chapter we have ideas for celebrating family life that help develop a child's self esteem, well-being and provide a sense of belonging, safety and identity. This feeling of connection, sharing and familiarity, helps us build an identity as a family too and that lovely feeling when we say, "We do this". Building history and creating memories have an importance for children that we don't always fully appreciate. Let them help to develop your family's traditions and you will probably find new ones emerge even if others are dropped as children get older.

Building family relationships

There is something about making the effort that adds significance to any occasion when family members gather together. Even if the event doesn't live up to expectations, the memories created will be long-lasting and binding. There is no guarantee that all family members will get along but creating the opportunity for them to connect can reap huge rewards.

Here are 10 ideas:

1

If you have more than one child, it's great to create some opportunities for one parent and one child to have some time alone together – even a weekend break. A friend of ours took each of her three daughters away separately for a week end together.

2

Wendy's husband watches one of their sons play rugby, plays tennis with the other and goes camping with their daughter. A group of dads all take their children and have a night away once or twice a year. They have great fun and it seems that sometimes it's the children who are in charge! The women who are left behind, pine so much they have lunch together as a consolation!!!

3

Where appropriate, encourage brothers/sisters to do things together so they build memories and share experiences. Even if the age gap is wide, an older child might be able to support a younger one perhaps by giving lifts or watching some sporting or other activity?

4

Supporting a grandparent's football team has meant that, even though there is geographical distance between grandparent and grandchild, they share something and can attend matches together and have post match debriefs on the phone.

5

One of Penny's sons encouraged his grandfather to record some of his wartime stories so they might be stored for posterity. The family now has a precious 30,000 word account complete with photographs.

6

Make use of particular festivals or events as an opportunity for extended family members to gather together. When Penny's cousin visits from America they try to organise a family reunion and invite all the family members on their mothers' side. A group photograph is a "must" on such occasions.

7

Take the opportunity to gather the extended family together for a weekend or longer so that different generations of the family can spend time together and develop their special relationships.

8

Encourage different members of the family to organise events so that you are not always the one responsible.

9

As children become more independent and move away from home, even if only for limited periods of time, new traditions may be established. One example is to organise a special family meal when a young person returns from university.

10

One family we know holds an open house for the friends of their children most Sunday afternoons for a couple of hours. This enables the young people to keep contact with minimal effort and the parents can also be involved.

5 thoughts about family meals

1

Eat a meal together as many times a week as possible. The importance of sitting in the same place with nothing to do but talk and eat is not to be underestimated. It can be even better in a restaurant as there are fewer distractions. Negotiation skills, laughter, arguments, heated debate, the art of conversation – just being together and establishing family relationships can be developed around a meal table. Not only does this help children practise important skills, it can provide a supportive framework for the way the family functions in times of difficulty.

2

A relaxed mealtime can also be a time for discussing your work and their school or homework topics.

3

Traditions can be built around family meals such as special restaurants or meals to mark significant occasions such as birthdays, anniversaries and the beginnings and ends of holidays.

4

As a working parent, the opportunity to spend time with your children's friends can be limited. Encouraging your children's friends to have meals with you can help you to get to know them.

5

Stephen Biddulph, author of "Raising Boys", suggests that once a child has reached 13 he or she should be cooking one family meal a week. This helps develop skills, connect with healthy eating and make a contribution to the family.

5 bedtime tips

1

Routines such as bath and story can really help prepare children for sleep.

2

Bedtime stories are very precious and make a lovely end to the day. Older children can also read to the younger children. This is an activity for partners to share.

3

Wendy let her eldest stay up a bit longer than his younger brother who is two years younger. It seemed to make a big difference to him and was recompense for the responsibilities he took on at times simply for being the eldest.

4

"Grown up time" is a concept that is useful to introduce so children realise you have a life that is separate from them. You may feel if you are working that all your spare time should be with the children but a great gift you can give to your child is the security of knowing that you are a couple, a solid unit, and that you like being with one another.

5

John Cleese and Robin Skynner in their book, "Families and How to Survive Them" suggest that if a child is upset or unwell in the night, the parents shouldn't move out of their bed and swap places with them. Rather, one of them should join the child in their bed or have the child with both of them. This we appreciate can be difficult if you are short of room or need a good night's sleep before the next day. The rationale is that subconsciously a child can pick up that they have the power to "separate" their parents, which could make them feel more insecure.

5 thoughts about photographs

1

Use albums to capture a child's personal history, such as the first and last day of school, showing where they were born and holidays. Older children love looking at pictures of themselves when they were younger.

2

A collage or album of their life so far is a great present for a special birthday such as an 18th, 21st or even 30th.

3

Similarly preserve videos of them as children.

4

Penny displays photographs of her two sons together on the wall and has done so since the birth of her second son. Under each picture the year is recorded. Once her sons reached their twenties, she was quite happy to discontinue the practice but there were loud protests if she even suggested it.

5

If your child goes to a child-minder or other childcare provider, have a special album for them to take with them so they have a reminder of family members and home.

5 ways to make birthdays special

1

Take a photo of them individually each birthday against the same/similar backdrop such as a door, to see how much they've grown.

2

Let the birthday person, whether adult or child, choose all meals on their special day including the choice of restaurant, if eating out is a possibility.

3

Encourage family members to regard the birthday person as very special for the day and to wait on them hand and foot.

4

Penny has an album of all the cakes she has made for her boys' birthdays – Wendy forgot!

5

Special birthdays may be an opportunity to collect sayings, advice, and memories as a present for, say, an 18 year old. If the young person is off to university or travelling this can be a wonderful time to have friends and family offer their words of wisdom – funny, endearing, warning or otherwise!

15 family Christmas traditions

"It will be a traditional Christmas, with presents, crackers, door slamming and people bursting into tears, but without the dead thing in the middle. We're vegetarians."

Victoria Wood.

1

Stirring the Christmas pudding is a very important part of Penny's family celebrations. When her eldest son was unable to get home to contribute to the stirring, she even took the mixture to his flat in Brighton so he could still take part. Of course there is always a photograph to mark the occasion each year.

2

Wendy starts the Christmas preparations on 1st December by reading a different Christmas story or poem each night, encouraging her children to join in. This still goes on even though they are so much older now. On Christmas Eve they always finish with "T'was the Night Before Christmas" by Clement Clarke Moore.

3

Build Christmas traditions such as buying a different Christmas book each year, or maybe a tree decoration for each child maybe as a stocking present. In this way children begin to build their own collection as well as their memories.

4

Penny's family has a tradition of the youngest son and Dad going to choose and bring home the tree. Although Penny has tried to go along, she hasn't been allowed.

5

Both Penny and Wendy planted a baby Christmas tree in the garden, which has grown even more quickly than the children.

6

Wendy decorates a tree for her taste and always had an extra one for the children to decorate when they were young.

7

Penny and her husband always try to buy a new cheap Christmas tree decoration when on holiday – America is great for this. They endeavour to buy those that have the name of the place and the year. If not, Penny puts these details on with a pen. She hadn't realised how important this tradition was until her sons went away on business and bought tree decorations back as gifts for them. As the family dress the tree they love reminiscing about the various places they have visited.

8

Wendy's children were told that the presents/stocking were taken up to their room after Father Christmas had delivered them as she and her husband never felt comfortable saying Father Christmas would go into their rooms.

9

To add to the magic, it can be fun to create the illusion that there has been a visit from Father Christmas, such as shaking talcum powder round large Wellington boots so it looks like he had walked in snow. You could also draw a reindeer hoof print shape with coal – outside of course! A half eaten carrot dropped near the house adds authenticity, as well as crumbs from the mince pie and a half-drunk glass of sherry or whatever the appropriate tipple might be.

10

Be prepared to be more upset than your children when they stop believing in Father Christmas!

11

Include the older ones in the magic of preparing for Father Christmas for the youngest children. They may no longer believe themselves but they can get so much enjoyment out of being in on the secret with the adults.

12

How about 'Grown Up Stockings'? When they're even older and want to continue stockings, have each member of the family buy three small items for everyone else. This way the parents get stockings too! Penny's family have been doing this for a few years now and everyone really enjoys it. If at home on Christmas Eve, the younger members still go into their parents' room to open them, big as they are!

13

Even the order of events during Christmas Day can establish traditions such as opening stockings in parents' bedroom first, have breakfast, then open larger presents left under the tree. The breakfast on Christmas morning can become a tradition in itself, with the family expecting exactly the same year on year.

14

As the children get older, encourage everyone to contribute something towards the main Christmas meal and take over the kitchen for a while on Christmas Day. It means there is far too much food but lots of days to eat it and everyone feels their bit is appreciated.

15

Boxing Day soup is a "must" for Penny's family and almost as important as the traditional turkey dinner. In more recent years this has been followed by a walk or a trip to the cinema in the afternoon and back home for turkey sandwiches.

5 other seasonal ideas

1

At Easter time a treasure hunt or Easter egg hunt for children can be great fun. This can be adapted to be inside or outside the house according to both the weather and number of children. Simple clues for the children to work out where the next clue will be adds to the excitement and you can make it last a long time. It's even better if you enlist the support of the older ones in the organisation and preparation. If you want to hide sweets or small chocolate eggs outside, choose wrapped ones in case it rains. You can have a different coloured wrapper for each child and they have to seek out their own. If this isn't possible then ask each child to find, say four each and bring them back to you when you will then share them out. This prevents the eagle eyed from getting more than their fair share and tears from those who have lost out! Have spare ones though just in case.

2

Bonfire night is a perfect occasion for establishing family traditions. There are many excellent public displays to go to as a family, which allow you to have much smaller events at home. Both Penny and Wendy have always done both. There was an expectation that the food would be the same each year with soup, jacket potatoes, sausages and fudge, parkin or toffee and mulled wine for the adults.

3

Trick or treating at Halloween has become popular in recent years. It is advisable to go to only those neighbours who you know will be receptive as, in this country, it can cause offence and may be risky. Where there is no indication that your children will be welcomed, it is best to avoid those houses. When your children are old enough and want to go alone, you may have greater peace of mind if you walk slowly some distance behind. An alternative activity is to hold a Halloween party with decorations, costumes, ghost stories with sound effects and games such as apple bobbing. If you want to make an effort with the food, Nigella Lawson in her book, "Feast", has plenty of ideas.

4

Families may mark the seasons in other ways. Penny has two sets of curtains (one set being really cheap and old) for the living room and changes them at the time the clocks go backwards or forwards. Apparently it is one of those seasonal activities that means a lot to at least one of her sons. Wendy rearranges her living room furniture so that her family overlooks the garden in the summer but are close to the fire in the winter months.

5

Include the whole family in seasonal gardening activities such as planting flower, herbs and vegetable seeds. Use pots or window boxes if you don't have a garden.

"In truth a family is what you make it. It is made strong, not by number of heads counted at the dinner table, but by the rituals you help family members create, by the memories you share, by the commitment of time, caring and love you show to one another and by the hopes for the future you have as individuals and as a unit."

Marge Kennedy.

Family holidays

5 tips on deciding where to go and what to do

1

It can be very useful to have a meeting before a holiday to ask what each family member wants to get from the break – even the little ones can contribute. Emphasise it's the adults' holiday too.

2

Consider the different age groups; the biggest boys can sometimes need the most entertaining – and we mean the husbands here!

3

We chose to have our holidays as pure family time. Because we worked, holidays for us were a time to "be" with the children all the time. We, therefore, didn't choose holidays where childcare or organised activities were provided, though these are very much appreciated by some families.

4

As children get older their needs may change which will influence your choice of holiday such as going where there are other children for them to meet.

5

Sporting and other activity holidays seem to ensure older children still join their parents on holiday – which may or may not be a good thing!

5 tips for preparation and packing

1

Writing down what you take on holiday and then highlighting what you actually wore can help with subsequent years' lists and save a huge amount of time. See Appendix B for sample lists.

2

Create a personal packing list for each child so they can begin to do their own. If it's a school trip, put the list in the bag to remind them what to bring back!

3

Split clothes across suitcases so if one case goes missing there is something for everyone in each case.

4

Put a label around favourite toys in case they get left behind (like Paddington Bear).

5

Wendy bought two of the same teddy bears for one of her children. One travelled with them and the other was kept at home, just in case. Another child's favourite comforter was a silk handkerchief – that was much easier to carry and replace!

8 travel tips

1

Penny's family used to travel long distances by car each summer. She had prepared something small for them after each 100 miles –simple things such as a piece of fruit or paper and crayons. This meant her boys couldn't wait to do the next leg of the journey and became very good travellers. It was a bit of a military exercise buying and wrapping the gifts beforehand, especially as she also had some for the journey home and the distance to their resort was 1000 miles, but definitely worth it. The worst gift? A book of 1000 "knock knock" jokes. She had overlooked the fact that someone else was needed to respond!!! As they grew, personal music players were a boon. Story tapes were also wonderful.

2

A tip for an aeroplane journey – don't start hide and seek – there is no end to it! Instead try draughts, battleships, noughts and crosses, dots and boxes, hangman, magnetic board games, card games, pens and paper, electronic games/music, books to read alone and together talking books, fuzzy felt shapes.

3

Pashmina, flight socks, water, rescue remedy, deodorant wipes, mini toothbrush and paste, are all useful things to have on hand.

4

A plastic bag on the floor of a car is useful if there is travel sickness or just general mess. A friend of Wendy's whose daughter was very travel sick found using a large plastic drinks cup with a lid, such as the kind you get from fast food chains, indispensable. Sounds disgusting but the alternative is worse!

5

For boys desperate for a wee while on a car journey, keep a large jar with screw top lid handy. Sorry girls!

6

Take some healthy, non-sticky snacks that are also non-crumbling and don't melt.

7

"One of the biggest mistakes parents make is to answer "Yes" to the question "Are we nearly there yet"? Don't lie. Use markers of time that children recognise. Say, "It's as far as it is from home to grandma's" or "As long as the Lion King". For older children, print simple maps of the route and let them mark sections of the route using coloured pencils so they can see if you are nearly there." (Paula Hall, Relate. Easy Living Magazine.)

8

At the time of printing, the AA website has travel games to download. theaa.com/arewenearlythereyet.

3 tips for during the holiday

1

When you have children, holidays still entail roles and responsibilities. Discuss these with your partner/other adults sharing your holiday. Paula Hall (writing in Easy Living Magazine) writes "One of the classic scenarios is when your husband says, "I'll do the driving, everything else is down to you", but you might prefer to do half the driving rather than being chief organiser and entertainer. Before you get in the car clarify how you are going to manage the children, so you have the best holiday possible. Mums often do all the planning, but that doesn't mean they should have all the responsibility".

2

Ask for help before and during your holiday. Check what's working throughout the time. Remember - one rough day doesn't spoil the whole thing!

3

Penny kept a holiday diary / scrap book in a plain exercise book, which was completed each evening, adding notes about where they ate together with receipts, postcards and tickets. Even in their 20's and beyond, these are still read and enjoyed by her sons.

Children's perspective - 6 ideas

1

Many children love to choose what they want for their birthday breakfast / evening meal

2

If the birthday fell on a working day, Wendy's children liked cards in the morning and presents in the evening. This helped to accommodate the parents' early commute to work. Despite having to wait, her children still wanted all the family together when they opened their gifts.

3

Children notice what parents do for each other on special days such as Valentine's Day and wedding anniversaries and while this may be surprising, it is an opportunity to model good relationships.

4

Children often like set meals for set days. The routine and familiarity seem important to them.

5

Both our families have happy memories of watching certain programmes or films together, bringing duvets down and watching a video, eating popcorn together.

6

Wendy has allowed their children to sleep in their bedroom on the floor for an occasional special treat. There was always much communal giggling – amongst other noises!

Child care

1

It is important that your childcare provider appreciates, understands and carries on the families' traditions joining in where possible.

2

It is also important that your provider develops their own traditions with your children. Children can adapt to and adopt different traditions quite comfortably, in different homes/situations. This can be beneficial in widening their horizons and understanding people do things in different ways. It isn't a lack of consistency — it encourages adaptability.

Spinning Plates

Mum's the Word

And finally. . .

This book has been written to help and support you if you are, or intend to be, a working parent. It's not about making the decisions for you. We hope you have found it a useful aid to spinning the many plates in your life.

In the 21st century it's the policy of governments of all UK political parties to help reduce barriers to working. For many politicians and law makers, the aim is a principled one of wishing to achieve fairness and equality of opportunity for all. There may also be the aim of maximizing the skills of the workforce. Whatever the predominant aim, reducing the barriers for working women is now fortunately main stream, so we no longer need to feel we are in the minority or fighting some feminist cause.

In some of the chapters we ask you to consider employers' perspectives. Pregnancy, maternity leave and the demands of young children on their working parents, necessitate that employers have to make adjustments which can sometimes be quite difficult. We suggest these can most easily be resolved through discussion and mutual understanding. While we think it's appropriate to suggest you co-operate in solving problems at work where reasonable, we are certainly not suggesting that your rights should be compromised. Actually, we think that if you, and others, make a success of being a working mum you will help change any out-of-date attitudes. Maybe then your children will benefit by having even better working patterns when their time comes, as well as having had a great role model. As hard as it can be, combining our many roles, there is much to celebrate and enjoy and we hope this book will help you to minimize the stress and recognize the benefits.

So... contrary to the title of this conclusion, there really is no need to keep quiet about your challenges and successes of...

Spinning Plates

Appendices

APPENDIX A

When things go wrong

Possible routes to take

"Effective people are not problem minded; they're opportunity minded. They feed opportunities & starve problems."

Stephen Covey

Things will go wrong – they would even if you didn't have children and worked. When difficulties arise, despite all the planning and organisation, it's more helpful to focus on solutions rather than believe "it's all gone wrong". It's just a temporary setback. Seeing it in this way will help. The danger is that when things do go wrong you and others may automatically assume it is because you are a working parent. Your attitude to problems in the past, your experiences, other people's comments, perceived expectations by society, all the changes that happen after a baby arrives, as well as your emotional responses to parenthood, may all have a bearing on your approach to a problem. The good news is we can change our approach and thinking to be more positive. The benefit of this is we reduce our stress and therefore we can think more creatively about the issues in order to find solutions. Be aware that the way we handle situations will influence the way our children are likely to respond in similar circumstances. As things go wrong, do ask for help. Do also make time to reflect and learn from your ability to manage problems successfully. Thinking about the skills and ideas you used will build resilience and confidence in facing any future challenges.

This appendix is about helping you to think about things differently as well as providing you with practical ideas and contingency plans. We pose some problems that may arise under each of our chapter headings and offer you a range of perspectives and some possible actions. Each thought, labelled a, b, etc., has a corresponding action point.

Chapter One: Being Pregnant and Working

1. "I've been made redundant."
Have you thought. . . . ?

a. Keep positive. This may be a great opportunity to take some time out and rethink your options.

b. Do you have a case for unfair dismissal/sex discrimination?

c. How might redundancy fit in with, or affect your maternity leave?

d. How you might go about finding new work whilst pregnant? What help can you get from your employer or others?

Action.

a. Consider having some career coaching – look on the web if you feel you might benefit from help in exploring options available to you.

b. Talk to your union/citizens' advice bureau/law centre/solicitor. You shouldn't have been selected because you are pregnant or have a child.

c. Investigate what the best deal for you might be. Your union official or an external advisor may be able to help. Your employer may well be happy to talk it through.

d. Take an honest look at your financial situation to see how quickly and how much you will need to earn. Can you get career coaching to help you search for work? Think about interim, contract or temporary work. If you are going for a new job be open and demonstrate your ability to work as a mother. This could include covering your current plans for child-care.

Don't forget!

You have rights, both as a pregnant woman and as an employee, which should be taken into consideration.

Don't let this situation spoil your enjoyment of your pregnancy and your thoughts about the new life to come.

2. "I feel I am being excluded from future projects because I will be on maternity leave."

Have you thought. . . . ?

a. You might be right. Perhaps your colleagues are anxious about your wellbeing and also about the success of the project without you.

b. This may be nothing to do with you being pregnant.

c. That this isn't something you need to be concerned about.

Action.

a. Talk to your colleagues and or boss in an open way to find out what concerns, if any, they have. If you wish to be included, demonstrate your commitment and ability, with due consideration for your pregnancy. If you really think that it is prejudice because you are pregnant, get advice.

b. Ask the question – "Is this really anything to do with me being pregnant?".

c. Satisfy yourself that it doesn't really matter and let it go.

Don't forget!

You have nothing to prove just because you are pregnant. You may be super sensitive at this time, and your fears may have no foundation. It should be possible to be kept in the loop without taking all the responsibility for a period of time.

3. "I have concerns about the person covering my maternity leave."

Have you thought. . . . ?

a. It is a relatively short time.

b. The responsibility to make it work doesn't rest with you alone.

Action.

a. If you are able, structure it so that key projects are on hold or managed in a different way until you are back.

b. Keep a record of all you have done to help them in preparation for you going on maternity leave. Share this with your line manager.

Don't forget

The work will get done and if it doesn't, this is unlikely to be all your responsibility. No one is irreplaceable and you will be able to re-establish yourself when you return. The person covering for you may make mistakes but this could well be a development opportunity for them.

4. "My boss is putting me under additional pressure."

Have you thought. . . . ?

a. It may not be true – you may feel under more pressure due to the effects of your pregnancy.

b. It may be true - to get as much as possible from you before your maternity leave.

c. It may be true, and he or she does not realise it.

d. It may be true – to prove some point.

Action.

a. Talk to her or him about how you are feeling.

b. Talk to him or her and if this is the case, work on plans together to cover what is needed and reasonable.

c. Talk to him or her to raise awareness.

d. Ask for what you need at this time. Be clear.

Don't forget!

Pregnancy will affect you, but remember your employer may have to make some tricky adjustments when someone is away, for whatever reason. People don't always realise the impact of their actions towards you and it may not be intentional. There may be some underlying issues. You need to take care of yourself as well as trying to understand the employer's perspective.

5. "What if I lose the baby or there is something seriously wrong with the baby?"

Have you thought. . . . ?

Huge physical changes are happening to you and they may have an impact on your anxiety levels.

Action.

Keep your options open regarding maternity leave. Talk to the medical professionals about any concerns you have.

Don't forget!

It is natural when pregnant to have these worries.

6. "Now that I am pregnant I am finding it difficult to perform to my usual standard at work."

Have you thought. . . . ?

It is possible but highly unlikely.

Action.

Talk to your employer about managing your workload at this time, if you need to. It may be possible for you to work more flexibly, work from home, delegate more, change your priorities and change your role, hours or type of work.

Don't forget!

In reality, your performance may not be affected at all. It could just be your perception. There are systems in place under Health & Safety and employment legislation to support you if you find you are having real difficulties.

Chapter Two: Arranging Child Care

1. "My child-care provider has left."

Have you thought. . . . ?

However devastating it is at the time, you might end up with something better.

Action.

Ask friends, family, student on holiday or a babysitter to step in for a period of time. Ask your employer for some flexibility while you get things sorted. Can your partner help to cover? Perhaps you could consider a different type of child care.

Don't forget!

You will probably be more affected by this than your child. Your temporary cover may require Criminal Records Bureau (CRB) checks.

2. "I am unhappy with my child care."

Have you thought. . . . ?

a. Is it serious enough for speedy action?

b. Can their performance be improved?

c. Do they just do things differently from you?

d. Is your child's behaviour affecting them?

Action.

a. If it is a nanny, au-pair or child minder you may need to terminate their employment. If your child attends a nursery, report your concerns to a senior manager.

b. Discuss your concerns with the child care provider, giving clear examples. Explain what you want to be done differently. Listen to their perspective. Further training might be an option.

c. Different isn't wrong and children can adapt to different people's approaches. However, if the points of difference are fundamental to your approach then a discussion is needed and you may need to insist that changes are made or act accordingly.

d. If your child's behaviour is the issue, sort it out with your child carer or seek some extra help.

Don't forget!

Be confident about your decision. Act quickly to remove your child from any risk. Be fair but make a quick assessment of your child care provider's capacity to improve.

3. "What if a) my child is ill, b) I am ill or c) the person looking after my child is ill?" Have you thought. . . . ?

This is very likely to happen at some time. It will be dependent upon the individual, age, severity of the illness and your judgement as to what is achievable.

Action.

a. You may need a backup plan in case your provision cannot cater for a sick child. It may be possible for you to work from home or take your child into work with you. Can your partner, family member or friend help?

b. If you are ill and you are unable to get your child to their carer, can your carer come to you? If your partner is unable to help, do ask friends or neighbours. Can your child stay with you?

c. A child minder may already have contingency plans for if they fall ill – check what they are and if the arrangements are suitable for you. A nanny who lives in may be prepared to still look after your child, if you take away all other duties. If so, shorten the working day.

Don't forget!

It is much better to prepare for illness in advance, so ensure you have contingency plans for each of these likely eventualities.

Chapter 3: Making the Most of Your Time Away From Work

1. "What if my employer expects me to shorten my maternity leave or work during some of it?"

Have you thought. . . . ?

a. This could be a good thing, as you may want to remain involved.

b. They may not have thought this through. Perhaps someone else could do the work which may be a development opportunity for them.

Action.

a. If you have had your baby, you could consider getting some part time help whilst you work, or bring your childcare arrangements forward.

b. Assert yourself. Suggest ways the work could wait or be completed by someone else.

Don't forget!

You have legal rights to protect you. This time is important for you and your baby.

2. "What if I can't avoid disruption in the house whilst I'm on maternity leave such as having to move or cope with building work?"

Have you thought. . . . ?

To remind yourself of the reasons you are making these potentially disruptive changes and what the benefits will be. You are likely to be around more to oversee the work but don't feel you have to do it all.

Action.

Look for help, whether paid or from friends. Choose the best help you can, whether reliable and efficient builders, a flexible removal company or a calm and organised friend— it can make all the difference.

Find a space and a place that you can have a break from the disruption, for whenever you need it.

Don't forget!

Your priority is your own health and that of the baby. As you are on maternity leave adjust the expectations you have of yourself and the level of responsibility you take.

Chapter 4: Returning To Work

1."I think I have made a mistake in coming back."

Have you thought. . . . ?

a. You might be right

b. You might be wrong and it could just be a matter of time or adjustment

Action.

a. Talk through your options with someone you trust and respect to think it through. Then talk to your employers to discuss options before you make any decisions.

b. Talk through your options with someone you trust and respect to think it through. Take any action to help the situation but don't act too soon.

Don't forget!

Confusing emotions may dominate at this time so allow for a period of adjustment. When you have thought it through, accept your decision and make it work for you.

2."Things at work have changed drastically since I went on maternity leave and I'm being sidelined."

Have you thought. . . . ?

a. Changes may be inevitable but being sidelined may only be your perception.

b. You may be being sidelined unintentionally

c. You may be being sidelined intentionally

Action.

Give it some time before jumping to conclusions. Your colleagues may need time to adjust to your return as much as you need time to adjust to being back. If you consider you have clear evidence that you are being sidelined, then share your concerns with your line manager, explaining your feelings with examples.

Don't forget!

Having a baby does not mean you are less able to carry out your duties. Have confidence in your abilities. If the workload seems lighter, use it to your advantage while you get used to spinning those plates!

Chapter 5: Working From Home

"This doesn't suit me, my family or the job."

Have you thought. . . . ?

It won't suit everyone or every work situation. You may simply need more time or to make some changes so it does work.

Action.

a. Assess whether you want to make it work and analyse where the difficulties lie.

b. This may be to do with your working environment, the impact it has on the family and the needs of your work. Negotiate changes where possible.

c. If you realise this way of working is not for you, accept it and consider the alternatives.

Don't forget!

There are many people who do work from home and you could find support by contacting them. Ask around and research.

Chapter 6: Managing Yourself and Your Home

"I'm struggling to cope with the demands of managing a home and I really can't afford any paid help."

Have you thought. . . . ?

What is absolutely essential? Food and health are probably the only priorities.

Action.

a. Ask friends and family for help. They may be very glad to be included and enjoy helping. There may well come a time when you can reciprocate. Depending on age, children gain valuable skills through helping and being more involved.

b. Lower your standards and cut out non-essential tasks. Maintain standards just for the aspects that matter most to you such as clean worktops, toys tidied away or swept floors. Decide what you could stop doing for the time being such as some ironing and accept a lower standard such as changing the bed linen less frequently.

c. How about having a skills exchange so that someone else manages some of your household tasks while you apply your knowledge and expertise to something they need?

Don't forget!

This could well be a temporary situation. You have nothing to prove. You don't have to do it all yourself.

Chapter 7: Building Children's Self Esteem and Independence

1. "I am worried about my child." (This could be a range of concerns such as, behaviour, being withdrawn, lacking in confidence or motivation, bullying, being bullied, a change in eating habits, pushing boundaries).

Have you thought. . . . ?

a. This is a normal part of child development

b. There may be a problem

Action.

a. Try the following approaches;

Keep the communication open. Be there and listen.

Separate the behaviour from the child when tackling any issue.

Ask yourself "whose problem is it?" If it is your wishes or preferred standards that are not being met, then think about it from the child's point of view.

Very often there isn't an absolute right or wrong. It will depend on the circumstance and the child's age and level of development.

Trust yourself and your ability as a parent.

Consider your own needs.

A useful model in having a conversation with a child about their behaviour is 'The 4 Part I' taken from Parent Link materials published by The Parent Network. i. Describe the offending behaviour. ii. State the effect it is having. iii. Tell them how you feel about that effect. iv. Ask them for help in solving the problem.

b. Seek help from a professional.

Don't forget!

Children will push boundaries and challenge – it is part of the process of growing up and becoming independent. It is unlikely to last very long but if it does then seek help. Talk to other parents to help keep your worries in perspective.

Chapter 8: Being Involved In Your Child's Education

"I am really concerned about my child's education or the school staff."
(This may be to do with poor performance by your child or staff, truanting or exclusion.)
Have you thought. . . . ?

You may have unrealistic expectations of what the school can provide and what the school can cope with. What is your child's state of mind? A display of behaviour that is unacceptable, uncharacteristic and not easily corrected may be a sign of some need not being met. The trick is to discover the need behind the behaviour, address it and, in most cases, behaviour will improve.

Action.

a. Find a calm time when you can talk with your child and really listen to their perspective. Ask what would help improve the situation so the extreme behaviour ceases and educational progress can get back on track.

b. Once you have greater understanding from your child's point of view seek help from the professionals, whether at the school or from linked agencies, such as the Local Authority Education Psychology Service or independent organisations. This is another time when communication is essential and good listening will help you understand the school's perspective and assist you in negotiating a "win: win" situation for all. If, however, you consider that correct procedures haven't been followed, do ask to see the relevant policy documents and ensure appropriate action has been taken. If you are still dissatisfied, ask for a copy of the complaints procedure and follow the steps.

c. In extreme circumstances, you may choose to educate your child at home. This is a huge step to take and your ability to provide an education in this way will be strictly monitored. Care should be taken to ensure home educated children have plenty of opportunities for socialising outside the home.

Don't forget!

This is likely to be a temporary situation and will end. Be careful not to jump to conclusions that it has something to do with the fact that you work. Most parents have anxieties about their child's education whether they work or not.

Chapter 9: Making the Most of Family Traditions and Holidays

"I have started to dread family holidays and special occasions in case it's not perfect or there are arguments."

Have you thought. . . . ?

Perfection doesn't exist except in fiction. Our families are not part of a Hollywood set. The media can lead us to have unrealistic expectations which can add further pressure. Family holidays are unusual in that family members are together for much longer periods of time than normal, so adjustments have to be made.

Action.

Consider your personal expectations of the holiday or event and whether they are realistic or not. Where does your influence lie? Think through what is most important to you. Is it about everyone having a good time, the food, or the look of the house? Find out what the rest of the family think, what they are looking forward to most and what is really important to them. Can you lower your standards or just not do something?

Keep communication open. Don't forget to say what you want too. The art of negotiating and even arguing is a skill and needs practice.

Don't forget!

Being together as a family is the key purpose. If your family is able to argue safely and make up, then you may be able to look back and laugh. It can also provide some good dining out stories in the future. One argument doesn't ruin the whole occasion. Remember these are people you love.

*"Trust yourself. You know more than you think you do......
It may surprise you to hear that the more people have studied different methods of bringing up children the more they have come to the conclusion that what good mothers and fathers instinctively feel like doing for their babies is usually best."*

Benjamin Spock

"Experience tells you what to do; confidence allows you to do it."

Stan Smith

Spinning Plates

APPENDIX B

In this appendix we include the following lists for you to fill in and use:

Essential contacts

Don't forget!

Christmas presents

Birthdays

Evaluating a primary school

Packing lists

Weekly planner

Plus a sample contract for an au pair

Essential Contacts

Services	Name	Address	Tel.
Doctor			
NHS Direct			
Asthma Clinic			
Dentist			
Optician			
Vet			
Local Police			
School(s)			
Childminder			
Hairdresser			
Garage			
Electrician			
Plumber			

Don't Forget!	Date
MOT expires	
Passport expires	
Insurance renewal	
Dental appointment	
Optician appointment	
Mammogram	
Smear test	
Pet injections	
Central heating check	
Smoke detector battery replacement	
Carbon monoxide indicator replacement	

Christmas Presents

Name	Gift	Cost	Buy	Wrap	Send

Example Birthday List

Month	Who	Age	When	Card	Gift	✓
January						
February						

Evaluating A Primary School

Area	Questions	Comments
The Building		
The Playground.	Is it clean, tidy and safe?	
	What is the condition of the fixed playground apparatus?	
	Is there a field, garden or other location for an outdoor classroom?	
	Are there litter baskets and are they in good repair?	
The Entrance.	Is it attractive?	
	Is it welcoming?	
	Is there a suitable waiting area?	
	Do you have an impression of what's important to the school by looking at the displays and by the way in which you are treated on arrival?	

Evaluating A Primary School

Area	Questions	Comments
The Classrooms.	Is your first impression one of a stimulating child-centred environment?	
	Is there adequate heating, lighting, ventilation?	
	Is there sufficient furniture and is it in good enough condition?	
	Is there sufficient equipment and is it in good condition?	
The Library.	Is there one?	
	Is it inviting?	
	Are there plenty of books arranged in a well-ordered way?	
	Do the children seem trained in its usage?	

Evaluating A Primary School

Area	Questions	Comments
The Toilets and Washrooms.	Are they clean, hygienic and reasonably sweet-smelling?	
	Are they easily accessible?	
	Are there enough?	
	Are they age-appropriate?	

Evaluating A Primary School

Attitudes and Philosophy	Comments
Did you feel welcome? Were you shown courtesy and interest by all you met?	
How would you describe the attitude of staff towards parents?	
How did the children react towards visitors?	
How was authority exercised and received?	
How did children treat each other?	
What did you notice about movement around the school?	
What did you notice about general classroom behaviour?	
What out of school activities are provided and for how many children?	
What links are there between the school and the community?	
How do children regard school? Ask!	

Evaluating A Primary School

Attitudes and Philosophy	Comments
How do parents regard school? Ask!	
How do staff regard school? Ask!	
What kind of parental involvement is encouraged? Is there a parents association or friends of the school?	

Evaluating A Primary School

In The Classroom	Comments
Is there a pleasant, working atmosphere?	
Are the children relaxed. yet purposeful?	
Is the teacher at ease?	
Is there a lively, stimulating and happy learning environment?	

Evaluating A Primary School

In The Classroom	Comments
Is there ordered freedom?	
Is the teacher able to get the attention of the whole class?	
Are the children enthusiastic?	
How would you describe the relationship between teacher and child?	
What is the general organisation like?	
Does it feel like a safe environment, physically and emotionally?	

General Packing List		
Item	**Outward Journey**	**Return Journey**
Passports		
Tickets		
Money & foreign currency		
Debit & credit cards		
Insurance/ European Insurance card		
Medication		
Phone & charger		
Music player + charger		
Camera and charger		
Plug adapters		
Toiletries		
Jewellery		
Sunglasses		
Reading glasses		

General Packing List		
Item	**Outward Journey**	**Return Journey**
Books, paper, pens, playing cards, games		
Kettle, tea etc		
Nightwear		
Swimwear		
Towels		
Outerwear		
Travel activities		
Sports equipment		
Baby equipment		
Other clothes – see example holiday list		

Example Holiday List					
Outfits	Top	Underwear	Bottom	Shoes	Accessories
Travel					
Daytime					
Evening					

Weekly Planner

	Mon	Tue	Wed	Thur	Fri	Sat	Sun
Break-fast							
AM							
Lunch							
PM							
Dinner							
Lifts Needed							
Notes							

Sample contract for an au pair

Welcome

We very much welcome you to our family and we hope you will be happy here with us. We will do all we can to make your stay an enjoyable one and hope that you are also able to practise your English.

The following are the terms of our agreement with you. We've put it in writing and we'll all sign it to help us both.

Job Title: Au pair

Main responsibilities

1. To take care of the children, Bill and Ben, and, in particular when you are in charge of them alone to be responsible for their safety.

2. To feed the children.

3. To keep the house clean and tidy.

4. Wash and iron the children's clothes.

5. Wash and iron your own clothes and those of the adults in the family on request.

6. To shop for your own food and, on request that of the family. To prepare your own lunches

7. To account for any money provided to you for expenditure on behalf of the children/family.

Hours of work

You will normally work five hours each day, Monday, Tuesday Wednesday, Thursday and Friday inclusive. Your normal hours of work are 7.30 a.m. to 8.30 a.m. and 3.00 p.m. to 7.00 pm. plus 'baby-sitting' on one or two evenings per week. You may be required to work additional hours on days when either of the children are off sick from school and during school holidays and you may also be required to baby sit for an occasional week end.

You will otherwise be able to attend college at other times and on the days of your choosing. Wherever possible we will try to ensure you don't miss college but we will need to rely on your availability to have care of the children or any of them if they are sick and we are both necessarily working on that day.

We are also happy for you to clean for other people during the day if it can fit in with your work with us.

Pocket money

We will pay you £xx on Friday of each week worked. Any tuition fees and travel and other costs connected with your college attendance will be your responsibility.

Notice period

You agree to give us at least one month's notice if you wish to end the agreement so as to give us time to find a replacement. We will be entitled to end the agreement on one week's notice in the first month, but after that you will also be entitled to a month's notice **unless** something so serious occurs that we become entitled to end the agreement immediately.

We would hope you would discuss any problems as soon as they happen.

Holidays

Except by agreement between us, holidays should be taken at the same time as we take our holiday. If you do need to take any time off when we are not on holiday or if you want to make some exceptional holiday arrangement, you must tell us at the earliest opportunity.

We will keep you informed of our holiday plans to assist you in making your arrangements.

Your holiday entitlement is one week's holiday (with pocket money) per 6 months worked. Any additional holiday will be by arrangement with us.

Visitors

We wish you to settle with us as soon as possible and encourage you to have friends, but for your security and ours, you must let us know in advance if you wish to bring visitors to your room.

Smoking

Smoking is not permitted in the house. This of course applies to us, to you and to any visitors you may have.

Car travel

Except in cases of extreme emergency for the protection of the children or any one of them you must not, without our permission given in advance, take the children out in any car to be driven by you or anyone else.

Registration

You have assured us that you have permission to remain in this country for at least two years with the right to work as an au pair. It is your responsibility to check if you need to inform the police and keep all the relevant authorities properly aware of necessary information concerning yourself and your presence here. We have the right at any time to require you to produce evidence of your right to remain here and any other matter relating to your immigration status.

Medical treatment

You will be responsible for making your own arrangements for access to medical (including dental) treatment. We strongly recommend that you register with a doctor and a dentist, and we will be pleased to assist you in making the necessary arrangements.

Use of telephone and PC

You have free use of our home telephone for a reasonable number of local calls, but we reserve the right to withdraw this facility if the number and/or length of calls appear to us to be excessive. You will be responsible for the cost of any overseas calls made by you as itemised on our telephone line, unless we agree otherwise. You should also be aware that all members of the family use the telephone line and you must be prepared to share this facility fairly.

You will have reasonable use of the family computer with internet access on request to us.

Problems

Any problems relating to this agreement or any other part of your arrangement with us should be raised with one of us at the earliest opportunity. We will do our best to sort it out quickly. If the problem is one which cannot be resolved without our making some adjustment to domestic arrangements involving us and/or the children, we will fix a time when we can discuss the problem together with a view to finding an agreed solution.

Care responsibility

Your responsibility for care of the children is one in which you must make sensible judgments in different situations in which you find yourself. We do however expect you to apply the following rules:

- Always be aware of where the children are, and with whom they are playing even if they are playing outside.

- If the children have friends to play or play at friends' homes, please check and be clear about the arrangements for collecting/returning them

- Encourage the children to be responsible for their own belongings, homework and duties.

- Etc. etc.

SIGNED: (All parties)
DATED

Spinning Plates

APPENDIX C

Recommended Further Reading (if not by us, by others)

Chapter 1: Being Pregnant and Working

"The Rough Guide to Pregnancy and Birth" by Kaz Cooke

Chapter 2: Arranging Childcare

"The Working Mum's Guide to Childcare" by Allison Lee

Chapter 3: Making the Most of Your Time Away From Work

"How to Afford Time Off With Your Baby" by Becky Goddard-Hill

Chapter 4: Returning to Work

"Back to Work: A Guide for Women Returners" by Diana Wolfin & Susan Foreman

"The Career Change Handbook: How to find out what you are good at and what you enjoy – then get someone to pay you for it" by Graham Green

"Killer CV's and Hidden Approaches: Give yourself an unfair advantage in the job market" by Graham Perkins

"Brilliant CV: What employers want to see and how to say it" by Jim Bright & Joanne Earl

"Brilliant Interview: What employers want to hear and how to say it" by Ros Jay

"How to Succeed at Interviews" by Rob Yeung

Chapter 5: Working from Home

"The Quick Guide to Working from Home: Practical Advice for Starting a Home-based Job or Business" by Hugh Williams

"Work Well from Home: How to Run a Successful Home Office" A & C Black Publishers Ltd

"The "Which?" Guide to Working from Home" by Lynn Brittney

"Working from Home Manual: The Complete Home Office Guide" by Kyle MacRae

Chapter 6: Managing Yourself and Your Home

"The Yummy Mummy's Survival Guide" by Liz Fraser

"Top Tips for Life" by Kate Reardon

"Nigella Express" by Nigella Lawson

"Jamie's 30-Minute Meals" by Jamie Oliver

"The Trinny and Susannah Survival Guide: A Woman's Secret Weapon for Getting Through the Year" by Susannah Constantine and Trinny Woodall

"After Work Cook: Fantastic Food, Minimum Fuss. The Working Cook – quick recipes for busy people" by Carina Cooper

"Trade Secrets: Everything You Will Ever Need to Know About Everything" – by Katherine Lapworth Alexandra Fraser Meg Sanders Annie Ashworth

"Time Management in a Week" by Declan Treacy & Polly Bird

Chapter 7: Building Children's Self-esteem and Independence

"What Every Parent Needs to Know" by Margot Sutherland

"Becoming Emotionally Intelligent" by Catherine Corrie

"Raising Boys" by Steve Biddulph

"The Secret of Happy Children" by Steve Biddulph

"Emotional Intelligence" by Daniel Goleman

Chapter 8: Being Involved in Your Child's Education

"Accelerated Learning in Practice" by Alistair Smith

"The ALPS Approach" by Alistair Smith and Nicola Call

"Help your Child to Succeed: The Essential Guide for Parents" by Bill Lucas and Alistair Smith

"Wise Up" by Guy Claxton

Chapter 9: Making the Most of Family Traditions and Holidays

"Families and How to Survive Them" by Robin Skinner and John Cleese

General Parenting Books

"Your Baby's First Year Month by Month" Practical Parenting

"Babies" by Dr Christopher Green"

"New Toddler Taming" by Dr Christopher Green

"The Sixty Minute Mother" and

"The Sixty Minute Father" by Rob Parsons

"Seven Secrets of Successful Parenting" by Georgia Coleridge and Karen Doherty

APPENDIX D
Websites Plus

The following websites are a small selection of those we think you might find helpful. Some we know and have used, others just look good. They are a place to start to get the information you need. For a whole range of sites for products, have a look at:

www.thesiteguide.com

Pregnancy

www.nct.org.uk -National Childbirth Trust for antenatal classes and support for new parents

www.direct.gov/ for up to date information on maternity leave rights and guidance. Try. . .

http://www.direct.gov.uk/en/Parents/Moneyandworkentitlements/workandfamilies/index.htm

www.babycentre.co.uk lots of information for first time mums

www.mothers.35plus.co.uk site for older mothers

www.affordablematernity.co.uk

www.bumpsmaternity.com

www.topshop.com

www.marksandspencer.com/maternity

www.Seraphene.com maternity clothes available online and in store

Childcare

http://bestbear.co.uk for parents and child carers

www.childcarefinder.gov.uk

My Big Buddy -male nanny agency

www.ofsted.co.uk for inspection reports on child care, nurseries and schools

www.gumtree.com includes childcare adverts

Returning to Work

www.gumtree.com -recruitment web site

www.direct.gov.uk Jobcentre Plus tells you about jobs in your area

www.businesslink.org help when setting up own business

www.lgjobs.com site for local government jobs

www.jobsincharities.co.uk large jobsite used by several major charities

www.womenatwork.co.uk network for women to promote their small businesses

www.hse.gov.uk - health and safety advice

www.skillsfundingagency.bis.gov.uk

www.womenlikeus.org.uk

www.motherswhowork.co.uk

Family Life

www.gingerbread.org.uk - supporting single parent families

www.ukpa.gov.uk passport office

www.bbc.co.uk/food

www.theaa.com/arewenearlythereyet - lots of car games for those lengthy journeys

www.activityvillage.co.uk for lots of tips on fun things to do at home and helping prepare children for going back to school after a holiday

www.mygonow.co.uk lots of interactive games and resources for children aged 3 to 6

www.bookthecook.co.uk Run by Karen Gordge who let us use some of her recipes in this book

General - Support

www.moneysavingexpert.com

www.bbc.co.uk/schools for online learning and lots of information

www.mumsnet.com

www.netmums.com

www.yummymummy.org.uk

www.community.babycentre.co.uk - active forum for working mums

www.momsrising.org - campaigning site for equality, recognition and fairness in the US

www.hint-n-tips.com tips from people around the world on a wide range of subjects

www.markfritzonline.com - for some of his inspirational thoughts, go to http://www.procedor.com/daily-thought.html

www.tamba.org.uk - for those with twins and multiple births

General - Products

www.phpbaby.com - products for mums and babies

www.johnlewis.com

www.mothercare.com

www.littlegreenearthlets.co.uk - for eco-friendly baby and toddler products

www.mumstuff.co.uk - for products for mums to be

http://parentlineplus.org.uk - for parenting support

www.babylicious.co.uk

APPENDIX E

Setting up a Support Group

Our Story

The inaugural meeting of our group took place at my house on 24th September 1981 following an article I had written for the Chiltern Branch of the National Childbirth Trust called, "Nappies in my Briefcase". In the article I suggested we started a group for working mothers. Seven women responded and a core group was formed. The membership grew steadily until it reached around 40 with a final regular membership of about 30. All meetings were planned by the members and related to their needs. The evolution of the group has been interesting to track, reflecting a growing confidence in women being working mums, and a move away from the guilt-ridden topics for conversation of the earlier years. We learned it was OK to look after ourselves and that if we did, our families would also benefit. The following shows the kind of topics we've covered since the group was formed.

Penny

2. The Early Years (1981 – 1990)

- Ailments common in childhood - talk by local GP

- Allergies in children

- Child psychiatry - talk by child psychiatrist

- Child-minding service and the child-minder's point of view

- Children watching TV and videos

- Domestic chores – how to cope!

- Dress party - clothes designed and made by two self-employed women

- Employment

- Financial matters - planning for the future

- First Aid - talk by Red Cross

- Holidays

- Husbands (we didn't say "partners" then!)

- Interviewing for a nanny / child-minder

- Job-sharing - led by a job-sharer at the Stock Exchange

- Legal aspects such as tax, NI, house insurance, health and safety, maternity rights.

- Literature pertinent to working mothers - guest Sarah Litvinoff

- Living in the South Pacific - one member's experience

- Microwave cooking (standing room only that night)

- Nanny's viewpoint

- NNEB course and residential child-care course

- Nursery education

- Organisational tips

- Partners were invited to a social evening. Conversation was dreadfully stilted, as there had been an agreement not to mention our children or our work. This of course left us with nothing to talk about! The funny side was realised after an hour or so and the atmosphere began to lighten.

- Promotion for women (talk by speaker who said, "I never seem to be amazed that women are penalised for having children but men are promoted because they have a family to support!")

- Relaxation (wonderful session of relaxation disturbed only by the loud snoring of the hostess's large dog behind sofa)

- School problems and how to solve them

- Second child

- Selecting the right school

- Social life of our children

- Social pressures (e.g. One member's neighbour had stopped picking up her milk from the doorstep as a gentle protest at her returning to work)

- Time for yourself - talk by a beautician

- Women at work - contracts, equal opportunities etc.

- Women's rights in employment

The Middle Years (1990 – 2000)

The intervening years moved the group further and further away from the more serious employment and child-care issues towards fun and care for us.

- A member's trip to India

- Acupuncture

- Ailments in children: - when to call the doctor

- Alexander technique (not a spectator sport!)

- Answering your child's questions

- Aromatherapy

- Assertiveness

- Book favourites

- Career changes and CVs

- Child care – living with the 'live-in'

- Child care issues

- Christmas flower arranging (convivial evening made *purrfect* by hostess's cats doing their best to thwart the presenter.)

- Christmas present ideas

- Christmas readings and shared supper

- Counselling and relationships

- Cranial Osteopathy

- Educational psychology: - when to call the 'shrink'.

- Equal opportunities in Europe

- Feng Shui

- First Aid – run by St John's Ambulance

- Flower arranging

- Gardening and garden design

- Graphology

- Hair Styles

- Holiday reading

- Image consultant

- Interior design

- Juggling act

- Learning styles

- Loss and bereavement in children

- Meals out

- Microwave demonstration

- Nanny agency - guest speaker
- Nutrition and allergies
- Opera is not boring! An introduction to "The Magic Flute"
- Orthodontics for children
- Outings for children
- Parent Network (the beginning of even greater support and help with parenting for several members on issues such as raising boys and sibling rivalry.)
- Photography
- Positive thinking
- Reading: how to help your child
- Recommended reading, films, trips out & recipe swap
- Reflexology
- Self-defence
- Self-esteem in children
- Services -all you need to know: plumbers, builders piano teachers etc
- Shared Indian buffet supper
- Shiatsu massage

- Stress management

- Tai Chi

- Theatre trips such as going to see "The Magic Flute"

- Toys – which are the good ones?

- Vegetarian recipe swap

- Walks to pub

- Wine. Talks on home-made and organic wine

- Wine-tasting and summer picnic

- Women's rights

The Later Years (2000 – 2008)

- Age issues. "It's their age"- discussion about children

- Artist talking about his work

- Bach Flower remedies

- Beautician and therapist: talk on current treatments

- Belly dancing

- Book discussion

- Books and software ideas
- Books, films recommendations
- Bowling
- Changing relationships with children
- Childcare
- Chinese medicine
- Christmas gift ideas
- Christmas readings and shared supper
- Clothes: choosing and buying
- Coaching
- Crystals
- De-cluttering
- Dependent adults – how to cope
- Desert Island Discs: members' choices
- Difficult people: how to manage them
- Directions: building success
- Elderly relatives
- Emotional intelligence
- Exploration of mid-life issues
- Family events: sharing successful ones

- Family tree: how to trace yours
- Fashion and Style updates
- Food- family recipes tried and tested
- Ideas for family holidays and days out
- Juggling act: - being a working mum
- Learning styles
- Literary matters: starting a book club; creative writing
- Looking after ourselves
- Money matters - help with financial planning
- Older children: how to support them
- Personal safety
- Personal training
- Photography
- Pilates
- Pimms and a swim
- Positive thinking
- Pub treasure hunt
- Recommendations of contacts, websites etc
- Reflexology

- Reiki Healing
- Salsa Dancing
- Stress relief products that help as well as for detox and sleep
- Tai Chi
- Teenage communication
- Teenagers: issues of the older teens
- Theatre trips
- Transitions: managing changes in our lives
- Tweens and Twenties
- Walks and pub visits
- Wills: and making other financial provision
- Wine tasting
- Women's health (menopause etc.)
- Working Mums in the 21st Century
- Work-life balance
- Yoga

Information leaflets

In order to support members, to sum up for those unable to attend meetings and as a forerunner to this book, we began to record information and ideas. So far they have covered:

- Child care options

- Home organisation

- Things to do with children

- De-cluttering

- Teenage communication

- Christmas present ideas

- Recommended contacts, websites etc.

How it works

In January, the year ahead is planned, identifying one date per month, the venue and topic. We meet in members' homes for about two hours starting at 8.15pm. There is usually a balance of topics throughout the year. See the lists earlier in this appendix. As well as the plan of meetings, we update the members' list. This list records details of name, address, telephone number and e-mail contact, partner's name where relevant, current employment and names and dates of birth of children. This list is useful for members to contact each other to provide mutual support. These two documents are e-mailed to all and the schedule begins. There is a nominal charge of about £6.00 for the year to provide funds for visiting speakers who charge a fee. About a week before each meeting there is a quick e-mail reminder to all members. It's a simple formula that works well.

One of our favourite events is the Christmas meal. We gather at someone's house, all bringing a contribution of nibbles, fruit and chocolates and before sharing a meal provided by an outside caterer, spend forty minutes or so sharing readings. Some years, members have brought along poems to read or extracts from a book. For the last few years we have read a whole work such as Dylan Thomas's "A Child's Christmas in Wales" or a traditional Mummers' play. At other times we have shared our personal memories of Christmases past. This has always been a well-attended event and such a convivial affair.

The group has provided a lifeline for members on a range of issues, supporting each other as children, careers and the mothers have grown. No matter how successful women are in the workplace they have still needed the mutual support and shared thoughts of other wise women – hence the longevity of the group and, we guess, the inspiration for this book.

APPENDIX F

17 favourite tried and tested recipes from Penny, Wendy and friends.

1. Parsnip and Apple Soup
2. Chicken and Pasta Salad
3. Wendy's Mum's Pasta Salad
4. Cod and Mushroom Bake
5. Pesto Cod and Vegetables
6. Penny's Favourite Salmon Dish
7. Baked Salmon with Onion and Tomato
8. Chicken Spinach Layer
9. Barbecued Chicken Casserole
10. Chicken Biriyani
11. Carbonnade of Beef
12. Spiced Pork and Lemon Pasta
13. Pork and Pea Curry
14. Quick and Easy Rice Pudding
15. Quick Fruit Brulee
16. Three More Speedy Desserts (fruit tarts, strawberry shortbread, meringue nests)
17. Fastest Ever Tea Loaf

1. Parsnip and Apple Soup

Serves: 4

Sauté 1 chopped med size onion, 2 chopped med size parsnips and 1 chopped med cooking apple in 25g melted butter stirring frequently until the onion is transparent. Add 1 pint (600ml) vegetable stock 2 tbsp (30ml) chopped parsley, (dried parsley OK) and half tsp (2.5ml) mixed herbs then bring to the boil and reduce heat. Cover and simmer for 30 minutes. Add1 pint milk. Allow to cool slightly before blending in a liquidiser. Reheat to serving temperature and season to taste.

Thanks to Natalie Ross

2. Chicken and Pasta Salad

Boil large bag of pasta such as fusilli or penne for 10 minutes. Rinse under cold tap. To some cooked chicken, add chopped bits of salad such as spring onion, peppers, cucumber, cherry tomatoes. Mix with cold pasta and a bottle of fresh Caesar dressing. Put in separate sealed containers for easy packed lunch.

Thanks to Karen Gordge

3. Wendy's Mum's Pasta Salad

Serves: 4

Boil a large bag of penne according to the instructions.Rinse under a cold tap

Cut into bite size pieces a variety of cold meats, salami, ham, about 6 slices of each.Cut 6 frankfurters into small circles. Add chopped raw red and yellow peppers. Add cut tomatoes (optional).Make the dressing: 1 part white wine vinegar to 2 parts olive oil. Combine with a teaspoon of tomato puree. Add salt &

pepper and a little sugar all to taste. Add more as needed. Add dressing ideally just before serving

4.Cod and Mushroom Bake

Serves: 4

What you do:

Put enough cod for four in ovenproof dish and surround with 250g mixed, halved mushrooms. Melt 1oz butter with juice of two limes, 4tblsp soy sauce and ½ red chilli thinly sliced without the seeds in a small saucepan. Pour over the fish and mushrooms. Bake for approximately 20 minutes or until fish is cooked. Sprinkle over fresh coriander. Serve with boiled rice and roasted vine tomatoes

Thanks to Karen Gordge

5. Pesto Cod and Vegetables

Serves:4

Roast small bag new potatoes (sliced) with red / yellow / orange peppers cut into chunks, 1red onion cut into wedges and 1 clove garlic sliced in a large ovenproof dish with olive oil and sea salt at 200 c for about 25 minutes. Remove from oven and add handful of black pitted olives. Place enough cod for 4 on the top and pour over some pesto. Bake for a further 20 – 25 minutes. Serve with fresh bread to mop up the juices

Thanks to Karen Gordge

6. Penny's Favourite Salmon Dish

Wrap one or two slices of proscuitto ham or smoked bacon round each salmon fillet and grill, turning frequently for about 20 minutes. Serve with new potatoes or mash, peas, broad beans or similar green vegetable.

7. Baked Salmon with Onion and Tomato

Place salmon in oven dish and scatter a sliced red onion and a handful of cherry tomatoes over and around it. Add a good few splashes of soy sauce and cover the dish with foil. Bake in oven for 20-25 minutes gas mark 5. Serve with mashed potato, jacket potato or rice.

Thanks to Edwina McKay

8. Chicken Spinach Layer

Serves: 4

Slice bag of ordinary or 4 sweet potatoes and par boil until just soft, then drain (you can omit this stage and cook for longer in the oven)

Cut up 4 chicken breasts into bite size pieces and toss in chicken seasoning (a tablespoon or so, depending upon taste). Dry fry chicken pieces in the wok until no longer pink (but they don't have to be thoroughly cooked) and set aside.

Layer half the potatoes on the bottom of your dish. Add a bag ofspinach (wilted if you wish but putting it in straight from the bag stops the dish from becoming

too watery). Pour over 2 tins of condensed chicken soup (add a little cream if you wish). Add the chicken pieces, distributed evenly. Layer the potatoes (don't worry about being too neat). Cover with some grated Emmental cheese. Cook in preheated oven on 180 for 40 minutes until bubbling and golden on top.
Serve with – nothing else needed!

Thanks to Karen Gordge

9. Barbecued chicken casserole

Serves: 4

Fry enough chicken pieces for 4 in some butter and sunflower type oil until browned on all sides. Remove chicken from pan; turn down heat and sauté 1 finely chopped onion until soft and pale golden. Mix 4 tablespoons soft brown sugar, 2 teaspoons made mustard, 1 teaspoon Worcestershire sauce, the juice of half a lemon, 5oz can concentrated tomato puree diluted with 2 cans water, salt and pepper in a bowl until smooth and then add to onion in the pan. Stir well and bring to boil. Simmer for a few minutes and then either pour over chicken or put chicken back in pan. Cover the final dish and place in preheated oven (170) for about an hour. Serve with rice.

Thanks to Gill Saidi

10. Chicken Biryani

Serves: 3-4

Marinate 8 boneless chicken thighs in ¾ jar of Tikka Masala paste for at least 2 hours. Finely slice 2 large onions and fry in a little olive oil. In large ovenproof dish, layer first the chicken, then the onions on top, then a large mug of basmati rice. Tip over a 1½ large mugs chicken stock. Put lid on and cook on 180 for 2 hours. Remove from oven and stir well, scraping all delicious brown bits on the side and bottom. Serve with tub of Greek yoghurt blitzed with fresh mint

Thanks to Karen Gordge

11. Carbonnade of Beef

Cut 1½lbs (675g) chuck steak into ½" strips. Heat 2tblsp oil and a good knob butter in a pan, add the meat and brown quickly. Lift out and keep on one side.

Add 8oz (225g) onions, sliced and 8oz (225g) carrots, sliced and fry till golden brown. Sprinkle in 1½oz (40g) flour and cook for a minute. Blend in ¾ pint (450 ml) pale or brown ale and bring to the boil, stirring till thickened.

Add 1 rounded tbs Demerara sugar, 1½ level tsps made mustard, salt and pepper plus cornflour for thickening if necessary and return the meat to the pan. Bring to the boil and simmer for 5 mins. Cook in low oven for 3-4 hours.

Check seasoning. Serve with mashed potato and a green vegetable

Thanks to Cherry Sowerbutts

12. Spiced Pork and Lemon Pasta

Serves: 4

Put 500g pack of dried pasta on to cook as per instructions on the pack

Cook 8 thick pork sausages (skins removed and cut into small pieces or use sausage meat) until browned. Add 100ml dry white wine and boil for a couple of minutes. Add juice of half a lemon the zest, a large pinch of chilli flakes and 300ml. crème fraiche. Season and simmer for 5 minutes. Stir in some parsley just before serving. Divide pasta onto plates and top with sauce. Grate parmesan over the top. Serve with garlic bread

Thanks to Fiona Shore

13. Pork and Pea Curry

Serves: 4-6

Dry fry 2lb lean pork mince and drain off fat

Add 1 large onion chopped, 2 cloves garlic chopped, 2 tins chopped tomatoes

large bunch coriander, 1½ tablespoons mild curry paste, ½ lb mushrooms quartered, 4 large potatoes cubed (skin on) Simmer for 15 minutes

Add 2 large cups rice, large cup of frozen peas and approx. 1pint pork stock

Simmer for a further 15 – 20 minutes.

Thanks to Karen Gordge

14. Quick and Easy Rice Pudding

Serves: 4

Put 250g pudding rice, 1 litre full cream milk, 1 cinnamon stick (not powder!),
60g caster sugar, 2 or 3 large pieces of lemon peel in a pan, mix and bring to the boil. Simmer for about 30 minutes, uncovered, and stir regularly. You may need more milk, and if you want to, add about 50ml of double cream once it is cooked.

Thanks to Karen Warden

15. Quick Fruit Brulee

Pour a carton of fruit compote - or a tub of defrosted frozen mixed berries – on the bottom of a shallow heatproof dish. Pour over a tub of Greek yoghurt. Sprinkle Demerara sugar on top. Put under a very hot grill until the sugar starts to caramelise.

16. Three More Speedy Desserts

1. Using premade shortcrust pastry tarts (one per person) fill with either mascarpone cheese or luxury custard. Top with a mixture of fresh seasonal fruits such as blueberries, raspberries and strawberries. Sprinkle with icing sugar.

2. Spread whipped cream onto one thin shortbread biscuit and add a layer of fresh seasonal fruit. Top with

another shortbread biscuit. Sprinkle with icing sugar.

Makes one

3. Meringue nests. Keep a pack of meringue nests in store for a quick dessert. Fill the nest with fromage frais and add seasonal fruits. A mixture of strawberries and passion fruit or strawberries/ raspberries/blueberries works well.

17. Fastest Ever Tea Loaf

Mix together 2 cups mixed fruit, 1 cup brown sugar and 1 cup strong black tea.

Leave overnight. Add 2 cups SR flour + 1 egg. Mix well and put in greased loaf tin at 150 for an hour and a quarter. Turn out and cool. Delicious for several days – sliced with or without butter

Spinning Plates

APPENDIX G
Helping others

How to Support New Parents

- Reflect on your own experiences if you have had children and offer the kind of support that worked for you.

- Offer to help with the domestic stuff such as ironing, vacuuming, hanging out the washing.

- Take the baby out for a walk so the new Mum doesn't hear them cry or wake and can get a proper rest. Unplug or turn off the phone!

- Ask the new Mum what she would most like help with. Ask for a complete list! Prioritise the list and put it up where everyone can see it so that each visitor can tackle the next item.

- Ask for a shopping list to add to yours when you go.

- Help set up on-line shopping.

- Cook meals that can go in the freezer.

- Buy baby clothes in a range of sizes – not all for new-born. Think about the seasons too.

Being a Supportive Partner in the Early Days.

- Acknowledge that she may be tired, emotional and needs affection. She may not know what she wants but do ask.

- Don't assume she knows anything about coping with a new baby – learn together.

- Give her attention and boost her confidence when she may be worried about her appearance.

- Be involved when she wants you to be – with interviewing childcare for example. Ask what you can do to help.

- Don't assume that because she is now spending more time at home she should be doing all the domestic chores.

- If she is showing the baby lots of love and attention, it doesn't mean she doesn't still love you.

- Being a working father means you can be a positive role model, but spend as much time with the children as you can.

- Don't delay getting home until bath and bedtime routines are finished. However, don't come half way through when they are calming down and get them all excited either!

- Discuss who will cover night time interruptions and don't assume it has been a quiet night just because you slept through!
- Greet your partner before your children when you walk in the door.

With thanks to Neil and Graham for their contribution to this section.